SINDH

PAKISTAN

AND

THE WORLD

a compilation of published & unpublished writings and interviews

ZULFIQAR SHAH

An ISM Publication

ISM
PUBLICATIONS

For the people of the world that cannot be
detached from its roots – the Sindh Civilization,
called also Indus Civilization

CONTENTS

SINDH-BALOCHISTAN-PAKISTAN

WORLD – A SINDH VIEW

BLOGS, INTERVIEWS & STORIES, BOOK ANALYSIS

SINDH - BALOCHISTAN – PAKISTAN

PAKISTAN: THE REALITY OF 1940 AND 1943 RESOLUTIONS

Pakistan: Politics of Fallacies

External perceptions of Pakistani politics and society are often fallacious. The analysis, policies, and decisions based on these perceptions, assumptions, and myths regarding Pakistan in the outer world are therefore often fruitless. Whilst the fallacies are numerous, by following BuzzFeed's lead and producing a top eleven list a picture begins to emerge.

Withdrawal from 1940 Resolution
All India Muslim League Resolution that was passed on March 23, 1940 called Pakistan / Lahore Resolution, was to implement in Pakistan States by founder of Pakistan, Quaid-e-Azam Shaheed Mohammad Ali Jinnah (MA Jinnah) according to which Sindh, Balochistan, Siraiki, Punjab, East Bengal and Khyber Pakhtunkhuwa (KP) had to become "independent, sovereign and autonomous" countries in accordance with 1940 Resolution. 1940 Resolution was to seek freedom and independence of the countries that were invaded by Britain after the invasion of Moghul Empire India. Such countries included Sindh, Balochistan, Punjab and parts of Afghanistan that became N.W.F.P (Khyber Pakhtunkhuwa now). India, today, is the Moghul Empire India that invaded Britain in 19th century, which later on became federal Union after Vallabh Bhai Patel, a freedom leader and Home Minister of India sought and received the instruments of accession to live together. India, although lost East Bengal because of Britain partition Bengal into Hindu and Muslim majority Bengal; however, half of the then Punjab acceded with India. The Punjabi along with Siraiki was Muslim minority therefore did not qualify to become part of Pakistan; however, on the insistence of Punjab Muslim League they had exclusive vote for the division of Punjab on the Muslim and others line. In the first round of voting the move was defeated as those wanted to divide Punjab got 49 percent votes against 51 percent votes to the opponents. After lobbying with a Christian Punjabi MLA / Parliamentarian of Punjab, Muslim Punjabi got 51 percent vote, thereby Punjab divided and Western Punjab became Province of Pakistan. Punjab was not initially part of the dialogue between AIML and Indian National Congress for the partition.

Much to astonishment, Governor General of Pakistan M. A. Jinnah's orders were refused in December 1947 against the "miscreants" the word used in the orders issued by Jinnah for those who killed Sindhi Hindu at Ram Bagh (Aram Bagh), Karachi in December 1947. The Partition of Indian Subcontinent violence began immediately after partition plan was agreed, and thereby approved colonial Britain by Punjabi Muslim from Hindu and Sikh majority districts of Punjab that later on became Punjab, India. When these Muslim Punjabi migrated to the Punjab that is in Pakistan today, they killed, plundered and raped Sink and Hindu

Punjabis and caused their mass exodus from there to India. This kicked off partition violence in UP, Delhi and East Bengal and West Bengal Borders. The December 1947 Karachi and January 1948 violence in Hyderabad in Sindh was by refugees of Urdu origin in which two indigenous Sindhi Hindu were killed. The migrations of partition from UP, Delhi and Andhra Pradesh (Hyderabad Dakhan) was caused because of Punjabi Muslim violence, rapes and plunders. Pakistan's religious extremist Punjabi establishment pushed some Urdu origin Sindh borns to have separate province. Why not, in that case, on the demand of Punjabi in establishment, a land in Rawalpindi or Islamabad be given to them? The 1940 Resolution ensures religious minorities' protection in all of socio-political, religious and economic. Until 1954, probably, there were Premiers (Prime Ministers) of the countries that are Provinces in Pakistan today' however word Premier has been replaced with the Chief Minister (CM).

Two Nation Theory
Two Nation theory is in 1940 AIML and 1943 Sind Legislative Assembly together. It is Muslim majority nation-states of the provinces that were invaded by Britain, and were countries before that. There is no "Muslim League Nation" entity concept as such; however, there was a concept of group of Muslim majority nations (Provinces) in the Indian Subcontinent. The collective identity according Sind Legislative Assembly 1943 Resolution is Indus Civilization's India Subcontinent's Muslim cultural identity based on subcontinental Identity that can be called Indusial nation informally however containing Sindhi, Siraiki, Balochistan, Pathan (Pashtun and Hindko), Punjabi, and Bangladeshi identities as "national-states". These lands have to be member "States" of the United Nations while containing EU like Indus Union as a "group". In these days, it is impossible for Bangladesh to become part of such group. In fact, it was folly of Punjabi majority and dominant Pakistan Army in 1970 that its waged war against Bengali people, that were Pakistani citizens at that time to avert implementation of 1940 Resolution. Could war with Bengali have reduced the seats in the legislature of Pakistan through war will Bengali people? The martyred Prime Minister of Pakistan, Zulfkar Ali Bhutto ordered forming Judicial Commission named Hamood Rehman Commission on 1970 war that handed over Government of Pakistan its voluminous report that was published during the 1996 rule slain PM and daughter of Zulfikar Bhutto, Benazir Bhutto that published in daily Dawn, Karachi, Pakistan; however some of its parts were kept undisclosed. Zulfiqar Ali Bhutto also dismissed in 1970 during his PTV speech the 1970 war involved Generals including two of his friends; however, he couldn't punish them for war crimes against Bengali that during the war were citizens of Pakistan.

Demographic majority
There is a much-touted fallacy that Punjabi is the demographic majority in Pakistan, but the demographic majority of Punjab and Punjabis are two different things. Out of 34 districts of Punjab, 14 are Siraiki speaking, four are Potshards, and the other 18 are Punjabi speaking majority districts. Therefore, Punjabi are a simple majority in Punjab and not an overwhelming majority of Pakistan per se; however, these 18 districts dominate and control whole Pakistan and its state and non-state institutions civil and military institutions.

Sindh syndrome
It is widely believed in Pakistan and abroad that Urdu speaking (1947 refugees that identify themselves as Muhajirs) are a majority ethnic group of Sindh, meanwhile some have notion that they form majority in the Karachi city. Such a tactical data manipulations of 'demographic fallacies' are created to underestimate the real Sindhi population, because Sindh has been dissenting Pakistani federalism and foreign policies since 1948. According to the census of Pakistan in 1998, the population of Sindh was 30.44 million. The ethnic break-up mentions in the census document that Urdu speaking were 18 percent out of it, which means in 1998 they were 5.479 million. Mujtahid Qomi Movement (MQM), the claimant of sole representative of Urdu speaking Sindhis (the claim itself is another fallacy), used to say that Urdu speaking people are a majority in Karachi, Hyderabad Sukkur, Mirpur has and Nawabshah. The total population of these cities, if combined according to the census of 1998, is 14.36 million. This means that Urdu-speaking Sindhis (Muhajirs) do not form majority in any city of Sindh or Pakistan.

Khaki truth
The majority of the military generals in the Pakistan Army since 1947 have been the first or the second generation of those Punjabi and Urdu-speaking refugees who migrated from India during and after the partition of 1947, and this is a major reason that the Pakistan Army has never pushed for a real democracy. Moreover, Pakistan's concept of security is based on geography rather than the population, which has resulted in the hatred of 1947 holding back any new India-Pakistan peace initiatives.

Islam and the republic
The constitution of the Republic mentions that the country is an Islamic Republic. However, as the history tells, Pakistan has been involved in the persecution of millions of Bengali, Baloch, Sindhi, and Pashtun Muslims in East Pakistan (now Bangladesh), Sindh, Balochistan, Khyber Pakhtunkhuwa and Afghanistan in the name of Islam. Becoming an "Islamic Republic" and acting in Islam's true and original sprit are two different things.

Civil democracy
The six-decade long process of the direct or indirect military rule in Pakistan has largely militarized almost all civil departments of the government, and majority of the nongovernment civil institutions in terms of their culture and loyalty to the supremacy of the military. There is, therefore, no 'civil' or 'civilian' socio-political and economic leadership in the contemporary Pakistan. There are only two things: civil of the military or militarized civilian leadership. However, those who have long dissented against the military establishment or opposed the very existence of Pakistan as a country (secessionist is mostly Sindhi and Baloch) have remained out of this course of militarization of the broader civilian fold.

Salafism and religious politics
Majority of the religious-political parties of Pakistan are indoctrinated with Salafi / Wahabi school of thought, but the majority population in Pakistan is Sunni-Hafnia Muslim. Paradoxically, the Wahabi parties are representing Sunni majority Muslims, meanwhile leadership of Sunni organizations, according to media

reports, prey victim of targeted killings in Karachi and Lahore. It is the real fault-line of the religious and sectarian terrorism and violence in Pakistan. In Pakistan, the few Sindhi Salafi there are, does not theoretically and practically believe in terrorism in the name of Islam.

The status of the Taliban
The Taliban, and other similar outfits carrying terrorism the name of Islam have never been and can never be the independent elements or nonstate actors. They are the proxy military of Pakistan, which misusing Islamic ideology are conducting warfare and violence for the strategic interests of their masters.

The Hindus population
Most of the columnists inside and outside Pakistan quote that Hindu population in Pakistan is merely two percent, which is one of the grand fallacies about Pakistan. Hindus, in fact, are more than 5.5 percent of Pakistan. The Hindus of Sindh form roughly 5 percent of Pakistan's total population. The problem with the official figures lies in the questions of the census, in which Hindus and Shudras (untouchables) are counted separately. The Hindus of Sindh, South Punjab, Balochistan and a small number in Khyber Pakhtunkhuwa together make up more than 5.5 percent of the population of Pakistan. In Sindh, Undo Population is 80 million.

Political tagging of feudalism
According to census reports, the large number of TV, Radio and Satellite facility holders are Sindhi households. Sindhi and Sindhi of Baloch origin today form nearly 50 percent of Karachi, beyond 60 percent of Hyderabad and more than 70 percent of Sukkur as well as around 90 percent of Mirpur has, Nawabshah and Larkana cities. If seen in that context, Sindhis are largest urbanized population of Sindh; however, they are new urbanites in comparison with the large number of Urdu speaking Muhajirs, Biharis, Bengalis, and Guajarati in terms of period of urbanization.

Due to these fallacies, the perception about Pakistan has been giving a different glimpse to the world outside. It is the only reason that most of the international analysts and experts on Pakistan do not predict the situations appropriately. Besides, this is the propagated manipulation, which non-representative Pakistani establishment has been doing internationally to secure it long terms single ethnic interests.

SINDH ASSEMBLY LEGISLATED FOR THE SECESSION OF SINDH FROM ROYAL BRITISH INDIA IN 1943

Sindh demanded secession of Sindh from Royal British India as a separate, independent nation-state country through Sindh Resolution of 1943, legislated on 3rd March 1943.

An untold Sindh and Pakistan does exist because the historical truth and facts are not made public until this moment to either Sindh or the rest in Pakistan as well as worldwide. The most important and precious truth of our last 150 years disclosed and unfolded today along with the evidences and details. G. M. Syyed tabled the resolution of separation of Sindh on 3rd March 1943 in Sind Legislative Assembly (today Sindh Assembly) is known in Pakistan wrongly as Pakistan Resolution by Sindh Assembly.

3rd March 19043 Resolution by Sind Legislative Assembly was moved by Mr. G M Syyed, the veteran Sindhi politician, and leader of the house in Sind Legislative Assembly in 1943. The resolution reads:

This House recommends to Government to convey to His Majesty's Government through His Excellency the Viceroy, the sentiments and wishes of the Muslims of this Province that whereas Muslims of India are a separate nation possessing religion, philosophy, social customs, literature, traditions, political and economic theories of their own, quite different from those of the Hindus, they are justly entitled to the right, as a single, separate nation, to have independent national states of their own, carved out in the zones where they are in majority in the sub-continent of India.

Wherefore they emphatically declare that no constitution shall be acceptable to them that will place the Muslims under a Central Government dominated by another nation, as in order to be able to play their part freely on their own distinct lines in the order of things to come, it is necessary for them to have independent National States of their own and hence any attempt to subject the Muslims of India under one Central Government is bound to result in Civil War with grave unhappy consequences."

In the first paragraph of the resolution demand the separate country-hood of all Muslim majority provinces in British India including of Sindh. Albeit, the Parliamentarians of Sind Legislative Assembly have mentioned the words "Pakistan" and All India Muslim League "Resolution of 1940" in their speeches during the discussion on the resolution." The word "Pakistan" was for the first time used by a Sindhi Hindu Parliamentarian of Sind Legislative Assembly Mr. Nihchaldas c. Vazirani. Therefore, word Pakistan is by a Sindhi Hindu, unfortunately the Sindhi Hindu in Pakistan, like other religious minorities are victimized. An ethnic cleansing in Sindhi is under way, Hindu are also victim of genocide. Meanwhile Khan Bahadur Mohammad Ayub Khuhuro mentioned the Lahore Resolution of 1940, which is called Pakistan Resolution.

The Sindh Resolution and Legislation of 1943 by Sind Legislative Assembly terms Sindh an independent national-state and decides to be free sovereign and separate country, and detach Sindh British Indian constitution, and also demand for other Muslim majority provinces I British India the same status. The resolution also talks of civil war if Sindh is not separated from British India by the Her Excellency Queen.

The Prime Minister of Sindh in 1943, called Premier, did not used word Pakistan in his speech on the floor and declared the Resolution as declaration of independence.

On the other hand, the so-called Pakistan Resolution of 1940 or Lahore Resolution asks for the semi-confederation of Muslim majority provinces within British

Empire's India Region as autonomous, sovereignty and independent Dominions. The much-toughed Pakistan Resolution 1940 aka 1940 Resolution does not demand a separate country of Indian Muslims I-e Pakistan; however, Sind Legislative Assembly declared independence of Sindh and demanded the same for Muslim majority Provinces in British Empire at Delhi. The text of the resolution reads:

Resolved that it is the considered view of this Session of the All-India Muslim League that no constitutional plan would be workable in this country or acceptable to the Muslims unless it is designed on the following basic principles, viz., that geographically contiguous units' are demarcated into regions which should be constituted, with such territorial readjustments as may be necessary that the areas in which the Muslims are numerically in a majority as in the North Western and Eastern Zones of (British) India should be grouped to constitute "independent States" in which the constituent units should be autonomous and sovereign.

That adequate, effective and mandatory safeguards should be specifically provided in the constitution for minorities in these units in the regions for the protection of their religious, cultural, economic, political, administrative and other rights and interests in consultations with them and in other parts of (British) India where the Mussalmans (Muslims) are in a majority adequate, effective and mandatory safeguards shall be specifically provided in constitution for them and other minorities for the protection of their religious, cultural, economic, political, administrative and other rights and interests in consultation with them.

Quaid-e-Azam (the great leader) Shaheed as he was known among the All India Muslim League members and their supporters, Mr. Mohammad Ali Jinnah, a Sindhi, talked first time for Pakistan by the end of 1946. Later on, when provincial elections held in British India in 1946, All India Muslim League was defeated by the G M Syyed led political party that formed the Sindh government.

So far political philosophy is concerned; G M Syyed was the first person who coined in 1943 on the floor of Sind Legislative Assembly the term "national state" in the history of political science having same meaning of term nation-state. He was the first person who demanded non-Dominion Pakistan States on the pattern of European Union.

Sindh allied Axis power, joined World War II and was defeated by the Allied Powers; unfortunately, Sindh was not made member state of the United Nation.

Sindh annexed by Britain with Pakistanis considered an occupied territory since Sindh was defeated in World War I along with the Axis Powers by the Britain.

Sindh no doubt is ruined, devastated in Pakistan. Massacres, resources capturing and genocides is over seventy years long political history of Sindh in the context of human rights, particularly civil and political rights.

PAKISTAN: ALL ROADS LEAD TO 1940 RESOLUTION OR THE COLLAPSE

All movements, demands, political discourse and human rights activism is nothing but the demand for implementing the Lahore Resolution of 1940, which Pakistan claims to be the basic agreement between and among the provincial chapters of All India Muslim League. Pakistan celebrates every year Lahore Resolution of 1940 as Republic Day. The resolution was passed between March 21 to 24, in Lahore, Punjab which is about becoming "independent, sovereign and autonomous" countries of Sindh, Punjab, Siraiki, Balochistan, and Khyber Pakhtunkhuwa (Bangladesh has already become UN member State) according to 1940, and has to form a EU like group (which for Bangladesh is impossible to be part of such group). The resolution also ensures protection of religious minorities in Sindh, Balochistan, Punjab, Siraiki and Khyber Pakhtunkhuwa in socio-economic, religious and political means.

Here are some glimpses of political movements in Pakistan:

(a) Movement for the separate country hood of Sindh and Balochistan or secessionism is based on their argument that the Pakistan (federal government) in last over seventy years has not implemented the 1940 Resolution that mentions that Pakistan provinces will be "independent States [letter 'S' is capital in the resolution] in which the constituent units [provinces] should be autonomous and sovereign."

(b) Although Balochistan was freed by Britain in 1947 as separate country before partition of British India, the Crown-Prince (Nawabzada) of Kohlu Princedom of Balochistan and member Balochistan Assembly His Excellency Balach Khan Mari waged armed struggle for over five years for the provincial autonomy of Balochistan in accordance with Lahore Resolution 1940; however when he saw Balochistan will not be given provincial autonomy he demanded separate and independent Balochistan. Pakistan authorities signed truce with once warring Tahreek-e-Nifaz-e-Shariat-e-Mohammadi (TNSM) in Malakand Division of Khyber Pakhtunkhuwa Province but it termed Balach Marri a traitor.

Jeay Sindh Qomi Mahaz (JSQM) leader Bashir Qureshi while seeing that after seven decades Lahore Resolution 1940 has not been implemented in Pakistan, he gave calls for Sindh Freedom March, and on March 23, 2012 amid hundreds of thousands protesters bid-farewell to the Lahore Resolution of March 23, 1940; however he announced to be bound with Sind Legislative Assembly's 3rd March 1943 Resolution.

Those Baloch, Sindhi, Pashtun, Siraiki nationalists who demand provincial autonomy are basically demanding the implementation of Lahore Resolution of 1940. Besides, political parties like Mujtahid Qomi Movement (MQM), Pak Saracen Party (PSP) Communist Parties and left-wing political groups also demand the implementation of Lahore Resolution of 1940.

Jamiat-e-Ulmai Islam (JUI-F) one of the two leading religious political parties also demands the implementation of 1940 Resolution. Meanwhile, Jamait-e-Islami

Pakistan (JI) has changed in last two decades, and they hoisted a Flag of Ajrak at Tower of Pakistan (Minar-e-Pakistan) in Lahore, which was built with reference Lahore Resolution of 1940. Ajrak is a piece of linen that dates back to Indus civilization Sindh and Moen-Jo-Daro.

Pakistan People's Party (PPP) without mentioning the name of 1940 Resolution passed eighteenth constitutional amendment last decade that inched forward Pakistan to the 1940 Resolution. Pakistan Muslim League – Nawaz (PML-N) and MQM also supported it. PML-N had also similar commitment with the duke-in-waiting of Khuzdar in Balochistan Sardarzada Akhtar Mangal who demands the provincial autonomy of Balochistan. Besides, Khyber Pakhtnkhuwa based Awami National Party (ANP) formed by Khan Abdul Wali Khan and Rsool Bux Palejo, and today led by Asfandyar Wali grandson of Khan Abdul Ghafar Khan – the Bacha Khan as well as the Aftab Sherpau's party also demand for the provincial autonomy. Same aspire the Pakistan Peoples Party – Shaheed Bhuto (PPP-SB) and Pakistan Tahreek-e-Insaf (PTI).

Only various brands of Taliban and Islamic State aka Hizbul Ahrar does not demand implementation of Lahore Resolution of 1940.

Pakistan Resolution of 1940 also guarantees the protection of minorities along with the development of their economies, cultures and traditions. It mentions, "That adequate, effective and mandatory safeguards should be specifically provided in the constitution for minorities in these units in the regions for the protection of their religious, cultural, economic, political, administrative and other rights and interests in consultations with them..." No doubt, the victimization of Hindu in Sindh and Balochistan as well as their exodus from Pakistan is against the Lahore Resolution of 1940. Similarly, the assassination and other forms of victimization of Christians, Shia Muslims and Ahmedia Muslims in Punjab, Khyber Pakhtunkhuwa, Quetta and Karachi is violation of this resolution on the basis of which Pakistan is claimed to be founded.

British India was a zone of Great Britain Empire, in which all the countries invaded by Britain were grouped as provinces, they were having their separate constitutions, flags, Prime Ministers and sovereignty. In Pakistan, neither Lahore Resolution of 1940, which ensured that the provinces will be: ... "independent States" in which the constituent units [provinces] should be autonomous and sovereign. After creation of Pakistan on August 14, 1947, provinces were not named "states". Although the provinces were having their constitutions until President General Ayub Khan's coup d'état; after Ayub Khan's dictatorship, provinces, provincial constitutions, provincial legislative assemblies and their languages were banned. Contrary to 1940 resolution, a unitary political system was imposed on Pakistan, which invisibly still continues.

Sindh area of Machko was annexed with Punjab in 1970s against the Lahore Resolution of Pakistan. Punjab Police as well as Pakistan Rangers – Punjab unofficially usually carries policing in Sindh.

On the other hand, Sindh Legislative Assembly on March 3, 1943 passed a resolution tabled by G. M. Syyed. The resolution reads:

This House recommends to Government to convey to Her Majesty's [the Queen] Government through His Excellency the Viceroy, the sentiments and wishes of the Muslims of this Province that whereas Muslims of India are a separate nation possessing religion, philosophy, social customs, literature, traditions, political and economic theories of their own, quite different from those of the Hindus, they are justly entitled to the right, as a single, separate nation, to have independent national states of their own, carved out in the zones where they are in majority in the sub-continent of India.

Wherefore they emphatically declare that no constitution shall be acceptable to them that will place the Muslims under a Central Government dominated by another nation, as in order to be able to play their part freely on their own distinct lines in the order of things to come, it is necessary for them to have independent National States of their own and hence any attempt to subject the Muslims of India under one Central Government is bound to result in Civil War with grave unhappy consequences."

In the resolution, Sindh Legislative Assembly said that if Muslims of India want to term themselves separate nation, they are "just entitled" for that. Sindh Assembly also declared Sindh along with other Muslim majority provinces of British India having "National States" of their own. If this does not happen, the resolution mildly warns Queen of Great Britain of the "result in Civil War with grave unhappy consequences." Sindh Legislative Assembly used word Province for Sindh with letter capital letter 'P' and word States beginning with capital letter 'S'. It was 1943, when Sindh took part in Second World War in alliance with Axis Powers for freedom of Sindh from British and was defeated.

In Pakistan, its founder a Sindhi hailing from Bhuj Gujarat in India, Mohammad Ali Jinnah was assassinated in 1948 according her sister Fatima Jinnah (please refer to Fatima Jinnah book on his brother M.A. Jinnah). The first Prime Minister of Pakistan Nawab Liaqat Ali Khan was also assassinated immediately after. This was following by the assassination of Fatima Jinnah. Some years later Sindhi Prime Minister of Pakistan Zulfiqar Ali Bhutto was also murdered. This was followed by the assassination of his sons Shahnanwaz Bhutto and Murtaza Bhuto. Mir Murtaza Bhutto was leader of PPP and later on PPP-SB, no case of killing was registered against him and his party members until his death. Later on, another Sindhi Prime Minister of Pakistan Benazir Bhutto was assassinated. The last slain Sindhi stalwart leader was JSQM leader Bashir Qureshi.

In Pakistan, either all roads lead to the Lahore Resolution which these days is known as Pakistan Resolution of 1940 or dismantling of Pakistan. Amazingly, those either demand the implementation of Pakistan Resolution of 1940 or have become separatist because it has not been implemented in Pakistan, sarcastically speaking, usually are termed by the security authorities there as demagogues of Pakistan and charged in the reason cases. Let the truth prevail!

-?

It is an established definition of terrorism amongst various acts of violence and militancy that when violent dissenters attack armed forces of a system, it is termed militancy. And, when acts of violence target civilians and citizens, the un-armed human persons, is unanimously called terrorism. This is general principle; however, there are other principles that falls in the various categories of a dissent or associated violent movement. Besides, the militancy or armed struggles that want to impose the political system that is against UN Human Rights Laws / International Human Rights Law like Taliban, ISIS/Daish and the leftists who want to impose Stalinist model of state which usually known "communism".

If seen from the session or territorial freedom movements' perspective, secessionists or freedom-mongers want certain territory to become a country. They own everything of that territory – natural and other economic resources; human resources for governance as well as social / private means; the state or governance apparatus of that territory and similar other things. Secessionism or freedom movements in the federations around the world since centuries follow this principle.

A session of a federating state or province is nothing but to declare it a country, turn provincial regiment into an army of that country, provincial / state assembly a country's parliament, provincial borders be converted into international borders guarded by the police, adopt a new currency and establish a ministry of foreign / international affairs. Independence of Pakistan, freedom of India, freedom of Bangladesh, freedom of Kosovo and East Timor are examples for that. Bosnia is the only country in the world, whose governance after freedom temporarily was headed by the United Nations although the state-apparatus was the same as it was before free Bosnia. Therefore, a violent secessionist movement does not harm provincial assets including human resources as well as system. Besides, provincial establishments use to have indigenous human resources. Any attempt against any form of provincial assets / resources will be against the political philosophy of secessionism / territorial freedom. The killing of Kashmiri Police in Pulwama therefore is an act of terrorism against the very much Kashmiri indigenous added that there are very few employment opportunities in Kashmir. The worst aspect, in fact criminality, would be if this act is by the non-indigenous, which means non-Kashmiri. India claims that this has emanated from the land of Pakistan, while Pakistan PM Imran Khan who earlier condemned it, later on termed it an "indigenous" act.

So far, Kashmir is concerned there are certain important aspects:

Majority amongst secessionist parties have political approach of a Kashmir for Muslim Kashmiri. They are not ready to include Hindus and Buddhist Kashmiri into their idealized "Free Kashmir" therefore the very notion of Kashmiri nationhood is baseless when it is selective amongst the Kashmiri people. They do not want a Kashmir country rather than they want division of Kashmir on the line's religions like South Sudan – North Sudan. In fact, their Kashmirism is an India-free Kashmiri land, not the Kashmiri people as an entity.

On August 14, 1947 Kashmir was not part of Pakistan. Viceroy of British Empire –
India region (Subcontinent) decreed creation of Pakistan consisting sovereign and
independent countries, which Britain invaded and included in their Empire. Lord
Mountbatten was still Viceroy of India, he asked Dogra King of Kashmir to choose
out of India or Pakistan, who in turn required the time to take decision. According
newspapers some "mountainous Pakistani" invaded Kashmir amid formal process
for the future of Kashmir during the British withdraw from Indian region of their
Empire – not from a country India. Newspapers also write Pakistan forces also
joined "mountainous Pakistanis" for the Kashmir. The question arises, if Britain
could create Pakistan, and their decision was acceptable to Indian National
Congress and All India Muslim League, then why their decision on Kashmir was
unacceptable to anyone of the both?

British Empire – India region, called Viceroy conglomerate of the Kingdoms, was a
conglomerate of independent and sovereign countries and kingdoms that were
provided governance connectivity so that British may rule the region and the
countries easily. And, that connectivity was Royal British India Army and Air
Forces; Currency and Imperial Railways. (Eastern Railway, Western Railway,
Central Railway as it had three formal name). Navy (leading armed force of Britain
and the Subcontinent), Border Forces, Police, Coast Guards, Parliament, Premier
(Prime Minister), national Flag and the Constitution of was each country was
separate. Remember, an Empire is a conglomerate of countries whose kings and
ruler accept a King or Queen as their Emperor; however, countries were given
name Provinces of the Great Britain Empire. An Empire is nothing but a kind of
grouping various countries under one Emperor. British rule in India was similar
to what European Union is today in the Europe. The important most question is
why Britain did not quit the invaded countries of Indian Subcontinent in same
territorial and sovereign country hood as they were invaded? Like Sri Lanka,
Myanmar (Burma), Thailand and other countries were withdrawal.

After Britain withdrawal from Indian Subcontinent, the first ever-indigenous
Constitution of India came, however the first ever written indigenous as well as
interfaith secular Constitution of India -- Aain-e-Akbari -- was by Sindh born
Sindhi-Moghul Emperor Akbar. Akbar was the first indigenous ruler of Indian
Subcontinent who ended the Mughal imperialism along with his Sindhi Hindu
Prime Minister Birbal. In fact, for the second time in the centuries' long history of
the Subcontinent, Akbar revived the Ashoka's Empire. In terms of political
philosophy of federal systems, the Indian leadership, Wallaby Bhai Patel sought
and received instruments of accession with the federation of India from the
Provinces, Kingdoms and their autonomous Princely states. India was named
Union similarly to the United Kingdom, Unites States and Soviet Union. Thus, India
in the thousands years of history of South Asia first time got birth as a voluntarily
Union or a Federation.

Unlike India, Pakistan had no federal Constitution far a longer period. In Great
Britain Empire, a Province meant countries whose rulers were slightly
subordinate to Her Excellency Queen. The Provincial Parliaments existed, which
in British Empire named as Provincial Legislation Assemblies however without
any Indian Subcontinent Constitution. Meanwhile the Empire's Subcontinent

central governance had merely two aspects -- currency and army and air force among the armed forces. Even Railways were based on clusters of countries called Province. Even today, railways in Pakistan, India and Bangladesh have separate police, judiciary, and administration, criminal and other laws. The founder of Pakistan Jinnah and his comrade Liaqat Ali Khan were killed immediate after creation of Pakistan. Jinnah's Sister Fatima Jinnah and one of Jinnah's close comrade G. M. Syyed were dubbed as traitors. Sister of Jinnah was also killed. No instrument of accession with Pakistan was sought nor was given by the Provinces to the Federation of Pakistan. The current Constitution of Pakistan is resolute (not legislation) because it is by the non-constitutional assembly, which was in fact a split assembly after the East Pakistan became Bangladesh.

All forms of violence caused or claimed by retrogressive or regressive ideology against anyone – civil and armies / forces is terrorism because it intends to reverse human progress by force against the uninfluenced will of people. Siri Nagar, Mumbai, Karachi, Quetta, Lahore, Dhaka, Delhi, Islamabad, Kabul, or Sistan-Balochistan or elsewhere, the acts of such violence are terrorism.

No non-indigenous movement for territorial session has been there in the human history. The current global values and international law only give right to the indigenous people to claim secession or territorial change in accordance with the UN Declaration on Indigenous People consensually legislated by the United Nations General Assembly in 2007. Therefore, any hitherto attempts by non-Kashmiris for Kashmir are acts of terrorism. Previous National Security Advisor of Pakistan, Sartaj Aziz said in 2017 that only indigenous Kashmir freedom movement can be successful, not the ongoing. Next generation of Kashmiri, he said, will become successful.

It is strange, that Gigit-Baltishan and Muree Hills are separated from Jammu & Kashmir in Pakistan out of that Muree is merged with Pakistani Punjab, and Gilgit-Baltistan since last decade is dealt equally to four provinces of Pakistan but is not given status of province. Still Pakistan wants Kashmir from India! In India from sub-cultural and religious point of view Jammu and Kashmir has three parts: Kashmir (valley) which is Muslim majority; Jammu which is thickly Hindu and Ladakh which is almost Buddhist. India never trifurcated Jammu and Kashmir like Pakistan.

Nehru tabled the Plebiscite (referendum to choose out of India or Pakistan their country), which is not a right of self-determination as such however it is a UN resolution way forward.

India is in fact in the best position today to toe the agenda of Plebiscite; however, any Plebiscite without merger of Gilgit-Baltistan and Muree with Jammu and Kashmir in Pakistan; end of all forms of violence in Indian Kashmir; and peace at Line of Control would be a drama. In fact, India should table a step-ahead to hold Plebiscite after above conditions are met, and should also toss for the space to all forums of social and political opinion given at least five years' time for engagement from both of the countries with the indigenous people residing in historical territories of Kashmir (in India and Pakistan). Whatsoever the results may be for third large economy of the world India, and the troubled time Pakistan, it would be the fulfillment of a promise.

This is the time when the fallacies should dissipate regarding Kashmir and beyond. No country, province or district of the migrant has ever existed in the world with the Self Rule. When Brits invaded northern America and migrated there, they became American and Canadians; when they invaded South Africa, they became Africans; and when they invaded as well as migrated to Australia and New Zealand, they became Australians and New Zealanders. In post immigration world, Vancouver is ruled by the Canada born Canadians of Punjabi origin that claim Canadian identity and are bi-lingual sons of soil -- English and Punjabi. A migrant cannot govern any sort of territory or administrative zone if not born on that land, and claim indigenous identity of that land besides, adopting the native language of the land. In USA, Canada and Australia both indigenous and invader-migrants adopted third identity together because the immigrants were basically invaders who won the war. Indian Kashmir has well maintained this; however, the Kashmir freedom claimants caused mass exodus of Kashmiri Hindu. In Pakistan, the migration of Punjabi in some parts of Kashmir; however, is a reality. Although born in the part of Punjab that is called Indian Punjab or East Punjab, ex-Prime Minister of Pakistan Nawaz Sharif is of Kashmir origin. He in Pakistan is known as Punjabi nationalism tilted political leader. Let the Indian should plan the return of Hindu Kashmiri to Jammu and Kashmir, and Pakistan re-united Jammu and Kashmir in Pakistan. Why the path of sanity should not prevail?

Terrorism, today, has no space. It has in fact enhanced the intrusion of state-apparatus over the society at the cost of civil liberties and social agencies. Let the Kashmiri society be given liberties by the non-Kashmiri whose acts of terrorism have ruined Kashmir, although they claim themselves friends of at least.

SINDH (JINNAH & G.M. SYYED) ENVISIONED A UNION OF INDEPENED, SOVEREIGN AND AUTONMOUS COUNTRIES NAMED AS PAKISTAN LIKE EU OF TODY

Pakistan today international and within Pakistan is known as a den of terrorism and victimization of non-Muslims in the name of Islam. Pakistan was not bound to be like this when it was founded, nor such state-system was envisioned by the founders of Pakistan Mohammad Ali Jinnah (M. A. Jinnah), his All India Muslims League and Sindh Muslim League. Pakistan, as envisioned by M. A. Jinnah in 1940, was to be European Union like "grouping" or block of the countries that are unfortunately called provinces in Pakistan. Almost 60 years before formation of European Union, Sindhi Jinnah's vision was to form such kind of union named Pakistan. This of his vision was resituated by a convention of All India Muslim League on March 23, 1940 in Lahore, which is called Lahore Resolution of 1940: The resolution reads:

"Resolved that it is the considered view of this Session of the All-India Muslim League that no constitutional plan would be workable in this country or acceptable to the Muslims unless it is designed on the following basic principles, viz., that geographically contiguous units' are demarcated into regions which should be constituted, with such territorial readjustments as may be necessary that the areas in which the Muslims are numerically in a majority as in the North Western and Eastern Zones of India should be grouped to constitute "independent States" in which the constituent units should be autonomous and sovereign.

That adequate, effective and mandatory safeguards should be specifically provided in the constitution for minorities in these units in the regions for the protection of their religious, cultural, economic, political, administrative and other rights and interests in consultations with them and in other parts of India where the Mussalmans are in a majority."

It was the first ever vision in the world, after United Nations, to form continental or sub-continental / regional blocks.

Meanwhile, his comrade G. M. Syyed was the first in the British Empire India who tabled a resolution in Sind Legislative Assembly for declaring Sindh an independent nation-state out of British India, which Sindh Assembly passed and declared Sindh an independent country. This great act against colonialism of South Asian history has hitherto never written. Sindh was the first province / country of South Asia that through its parliament declared itself a country outside British Empire, and was second country after America that separated itself from British Empire. This has not been mentioned in our human history. This Sind Legislative Assembly resolution of March 3, 1943 reads:

"This House recommends to Government to convey to His Majesty's Government through His Excellency the Viceroy, the sentiments and wishes of the Muslims of this Province that whereas Muslims of India are a separate nation possessing religion, philosophy, social customs, literature, traditions, political and economic theories of their own, quite different from those of the Hindus, they are justly entitled to the right, as a single, separate nation, to have independent national states of their own, carved out in the zones where they are in majority in the sub-continent of India.

Wherefore they emphatically declare that no constitution shall be acceptable to them that will place the Muslims under a Central Government dominated by another nation, as in order to be able to play their part freely on their own distinct lines in the order of things to come, it is necessary for them to have independent National States of their own and hence any attempt to subject the Muslims of India under one Central Government is bound to result in Civil War with grave unhappy consequences." (Proceedings of the Sindh Legislative Assembly, Official Report, Vol. XVII-No.6, Wednesday 3rd March, 1943, Karachi on www.pas.gov.pk)

Sindh through Sindh Army also joined Second World War and had alliance with Axis Forces under Pir Pagaro Sorihya Badshah in 1942-43. At the same time, India (Hind) also joined the war and allied with Axis Forces under Netaji Subhash Chandra Bose and Indian National Army (INA). A Sindhi of Punjabi origin Molana

Obaidullah Sindhi was civil leader of Government of India in Exile at Kabul, Afghanistan. He was Home Minister of the Government of Exile and Netaji Subash Chandra Bose was Commander of INA. Sindh and Hind (India) lost the war against Great Britain. This chapter of world as well as South Asian history has not been narrated in fullest. In Sindh and Hind wars against British Empire, Sindh Army could liberate district Sangha for one year and formed government named Sangha Sarkar that was having ministries, taxation system and judiciary that filled again to Britain.

Since Sindh, Balochistan, Siraiki Southern Punjab (Pakistan), Gujarat, Rajasthan (India) Helmand (Afghanistan) and Sistan-Balochistan (Iran) are one people since thousands of years; however, Sindhi in Pakistan claim Sindh as a country, Balochistani claim Balochistan country; and Siraiki claim Siraiki Wasey, Siraiki homeland. The recent USA banned Baloch Liberation Army (BLA) have claimed Balochistan that is in Pakistan their country. G. M. Syyed, on the floor of Sind Assembly during the declaration of Sind Legislative Assembly on March 3, 1943 said, "After this general survey of more or less homogeneous and geographically, socially, economically, religiously, politically one people and yet impossible either to unite or be governed as one national unit, let us revert to Indian conditions. I have already pointed out the impossibility of considering 2 provinces in India, say, like Sind and Gujrat, not to speak of Bengal, Central provinces, Madras etc. as one geographical unit." He clearly meant that Sind and Rajasthan are not part of 1943's Sindh and the declaration of independence of Sindh was only for Sindh alone being based on Muslim majority Sindh's Sindhi nation of all religion Sindhi. Sindh, Gujarat and Rajasthan ethno-linguistically are same people who talk riverine Sindhi dialect, Marwari and Dhaka desert dialect, Kathiawar and Gujarati dialects. Meanwhile Sindhi and Baloch are same people who talk riverine Sindh, Balochi, Brahmi and Siraiki. The same is for Sistan-Balochistan province in Iran and Helmand province in Balochistan. Similar is Khorasan province in Iran.

Besides, Rajasthani and Sindhi migrated from today's Sindh and Rajasthan some centuries ago to the Newar and other areas of Nepal. At least twenty percent of ethno-linguistic fabric of Nepali is of Sindh-Rajasthani origin, almost 32 clans in Nepal are of today's Sindh and Rajasthan origin that also includes Mullah, Sarki, Pali, Rajput and others. Over 20 percent vocabulary of Nepali is same as in Sindhi and Rajasthani. The Nepali phonetics is similar to ancient Sindhi language. A Sindhi, if listens Nepali slowly, does not need translation. There are at least two old places in Nepal called Sindhu Pal Chowk and Sindhu Pal Road. According to Nepali Scholar Kanak Mani Dixit, this is because of Indus civilization and historical migration from Rajasthan to Sindh. Besides, scholar and PhD in Linguistics, Dr. Mani Dixit, the ex-Duke of Pattan Dhoka, Kathmandu, the great aspect of Sindhi-Nepali similarity is the phonetics of both of the languages.

Meanwhile, Kurds, according to the established Kurd and Balochistan-History, Kurd tribe of Sindh Indus migrated to today's "Kurdistan in 1 Century BC" (mentions book, A People Without Country). On the other hand, Roma people Europe, that are called Sinti in Germany claim that they are from centuries old Sindh Kingdom.

After this general survey of more or less homogeneous and geographically, socially, economically, religiously, politically one people and yet impossible either to unite or be governed as one national unit, let us revert to Indian conditions. I have already pointed out the impossibility of considering 2 provinces in India, say, like Sind and Gujrat, not to speak of Bengal, Central provinces, Madras etc. as one geographical unit.

In the contemporary times, China's ambitious One Road, One Belt (OBOR) plan, a road, maritime and railways infrastructure network that would encompass sixty countries and will require the infrastructure investment of US\$ 4 to 8 trillion. Chinese President Xi Jinping falsely claim this continuation China's historical Silk Route.

SILK ROUTE, SINDH AND RESOLUTIONS OF 1940 AND 1943

Historically Silk Route belongs to Sindh, which for centuries China, Afghanistan, today's India, Central Asia and Russia were using for the trade. This truth is well document in the books of history and are available in the Oxford University Press, UK's published books' catalogues. in fact, China should mention it historical One Belt One Road of Kingdom of Sindh. The slain ex-Prime Minister of Pakistan Benazir Bhutto, a Sindhi, wanted this re-initiate this historical One Belt, One Route of Sindh in 1996, named it Keti Bandar Project, Punjab security establishment of Pakistan forced to rejected this. Later on, all of sudden China's Xi Jinping came with the same idea and earned status of Mao Zedong in the Communist Party of China due to Sindh's historical by claiming the concept of One Belt, One Road / Silk Route.

The central governments of Pakistan and China have signed Agreements / MoUs regarding the road as well as the Port of Gwadar under the China Pakistan economic Corridor (CPEC), against the will and interest of Indigenous Sindhi, Baloch, Pathan, and Siraiki which has caused genocide, crimes against humanity, and war crimes by ethnic-Punjabi

Pakistan was to be a EU like "group" of the sovereign, independent and autonomous States (countries) according to the Resolution of 1940 by All India Muslim League (AIML), which Pakistan claims to be the document on which Republic of Pakistan, came into existence   however the decolonization process was not and has not been materialized since December 1947, and has become illegitimately a single country since 22nd November 1954 through terming countries in Pakistan into districts / provinces, which later on further skewed through the constitution by the military rule of General Ayub Khan in 1962, which was and is against the Partition Plan of Indian Subcontinent agreed by the founders of Pakistan M. A. Jinnah and Liaqat Ali Khan, leaders of the then All India Muslim League (AIML) in early 1947. The plan was endorsed by colonial Great Britain Empire (GB) Her Royal Majesty, the Queen, through her royal governor general then called Viceroy -- His Royal Majesty Lord Mountbatten. Since Governor General of Pakistan M. A. Jinnah succeeded H.R.M Viceroy British Indian Subcontinent for Sindh, Siraiki, Punjab, and Khyber Pakhtunkhuwa (then called N.W.F.P) together called Pakistan and was meant to process the decolonization process in the light above mentioned 1940 Resolution with the coordination by

Governor General M.A. Jinnah through the Governors of these "independent, autonomous and sovereign" countries and their governments led by a Primer of each excluding Siraiki whose King (Nawab) hand throne at Bahawalpur. Meanwhile, Balochistan was declared an independent, autonomous and sovereign country before Pakistan process that began through transfer of power to M. A. Jinnah on 14th August 1947 by H.R.M. Queen of GB. He, although, was made powerless in December 1947 by Punjabi army, called Punjab Regiment before 1947 and later on became Pakistan Army by merger of a small numbered Regiment of Frontier Force. According to M. A. Jinnah's sister Fatima Jinnah, entitled a Mother of the Peoples in Pakistan, wrote that his brother M. A, Jinnah was assassinated (Kindly refer to his book "My Brother" 1987 edition -- some parts of the book are censured in Pakistan recently). She herself was killed under military rule in Pakistan, Ayub Khan according to Petition by one Ghulam Sarwar under section 176 of Criminal Procedures before Additional City Magistrate Mumtaz Muhammad Baig according to "How Fatima Jinnah died", Daily Dawn, Karachi, Pakistan, www.dawn.com/news/1159181 . The same is express by a senior Pakistan bureaucrat Qutubdin Shahab in his Book "Shahabnama" (Kindly refer to Urdu book edition in 1980s. Balochistan was invaded by above mentioned Pakistan Army without orders by M. A. Jinnah, like before that Kashmir was invaded in December 1947. Furthermore, Sindh Legislative Assembly, in 1943, led by the then Premier of Sindh Ghulam Hussain Hidayatullah, and leader of Sindh Muslim League G. M. Syyed declared Sindh a country outside colonial British Empire and a "national state" today a Province in Pakistan. Besides, the Constitution of Pakistan of 1973 was made by a non-constitutional assembly that terms Pakistan a Federation. Khyber Pakhtunkhuwa, Balochistan, Sindh, Siraiki and Punjab are not made independent, sovereign and autonomous countries in accordance AIML Pakistan Resolution of 1940 and Sind Legislative Assembly Resolution of 3rd March 1943 under the Declaration on the Granting of Independence to Colonial Countries and People, legislated through UN General Assembly Resolution 1514 (XV) of 14th December 1960. Therefore, ICC has a jurisdiction in this matter.

The systematic genocide due to the China Pakistan Economic Cordon (CPEC) by ethnic Punjabi origin authorities mainly form powerful security regime of Pakistan hailing from Punjabi speaking districts of Punjab in Pakistan through both a. economic woes for the people of Gilgit Baltistan-Kashmir in the form of procedural ban on tourism, the only source of living there fishing communities in Gwadar, and others in Balochistan, and Sindh and was rejected by Tribal Assembly called "Jirga" and b. increase in drastic human rights violation as well as crime against humanity that falls under the ambit of Article 7 (e, h, k) of the Part 2, Rome Statute of the International Criminal Court. Besides, Chinese Navy's presence at Balochistan Coast around Gwadar is violation of United Nations Declaration of Indigenous People 31 and 31 and is also violation of Rome Statute's genocide, crimes against humanity and war crimes parts with reference to adverse impacts of Chinese Navy presence at Balochistan and Sindh coast without the will of Balochistani and Sindhi on the indigenous people of Balochistan in terms of their collective psyche health, their interests, right on their indigenous land as well costal resources, economy and livelihood, and drag them into international conflicts like situation at the junction of Straight of Hamoz and Arabian Sea. The evidences and details of these can be sought from the human rights bodies like World Sindhi Congress, Amnesty International, and the Office of the High Commissioner on Human Rights, UN, Geneva. Besides, Since, above mentioned Pakistan authorities, during military rule of Pakistan Army Chief General Pervez Musharaf Balochistani engaged with the Government for handing over the authorities of Shipping of Ports Ministry back to Balochistan like these were with the province during colonial era of British Empire, and were also with Balochistan before military rule of President General Ayub Khan besides seeking further guarantees regarding population shift, mainly of ethnic Punjabi, to Gwadar that would turn indigenous Baloch into minority in Balochistan. The authorities refused despite insurrected the Balochistan Assembly member as well as one of the Princes of Balochistan Nawab Balach Khan Marri. Nawab Balach, in response, incept war for Balochistan through quoting 1940 Resolution in his words "Provincial autonomy" as well as for his motherland Balochistan. This has caused injuries and death of thousands of civilian Baloch through various means through ground as well as airborne troops on the orders of military ruler President General Pervez Musharaf. Musharaf, although was of Urdu origin, however this served the ethno-national Punjabi majority security establishment of Pakistan. The situation kept is still underway. Ethnic Punjabi that is a dominant majority in Pakistan's military and security regime is also involved in Taliban, Al-Qaida, ISIS and other kinds of attempt to invasion Afghanistan, terrorism and crimes against humanity including war crimes in Afghanistan, USA, Sri Lanka, Sindh, Balochistan, Siraiki and Punjabi lands in Punjab and KP provinces in Pakistan including Gilgit-Baltistan-Kashmir besides, Iran, Central Asian countries, Russia, Europe, Africa, and Asia-Pacific region. This global terrorism and genocide of various nations, religions, sects and ethnic origin people has caused deaths of thousands of the innocent civilians. Recently USA State Department has declared the above mentioned Nawab Balach Marri led Balochistan War's Baloch Liberation Army (BLA) a global terrorist organization; however while doing this USA authorities have violated and went against the bellow mentioned international legal instruments, besides acting against M. A. Jinnah and Liaqat Ali Khan's agreed Partition of India (Subcontinent) Plan in accordance with All India Muslim League's 1940 as well as decolonization by colonial British Empire's Royal authorities through formally declaring Balochistan an independent, sovereign and autonomous country, which is fundamentally violation of Declaration on the Granting of Independence to Colonial Countries and People, legislated through UN General Assembly Resolution 1514 (XV) of 14th December 1960. The details regarding above all can be got from BBC Radio Urdu Service achieves in the forms of reports of the then BBC Reporter in Sindh, Pakistan Mark Tully; World Sindhi Congress and Office of the High Commissioner on Human Rights, UN, Geneva. Furthermore, the unmilitary aggression by ethnic Punjabi majority armed forces on the civilian of Sindh equalant to war crime as per Article 8, 2 a (I) when Sindhi and a Baloch activist was burnt alive through the use of chemical weapons. The details of which can be got from link a human rights investigation report on burning alive of three men in Sindh, Pakistan. The honorable court can also / or consider this an act of genocide. Meanwhile, under CPEC Government of China has not signed MoUs / Agreements with Sindh, Balochistan, Siraiki (southern Punjab) through Nawab of Bahawalpur; Khyber Pakhtunkhuwa and Gilgit-Baltistan-Kashmir. The current President of China, against the historical realities, has falsely claimed that historical Silk Route is of China and has named it One Belt One Road-CPEC. Sindh's historical Silk Route that is over 5000 years old and formally ceased to exist to greater extent in 1917 after communist revolution Tsarist Russia; however partly carried its operations until 2014. In pre-historical era its headquarters was Moen-Jo-Daro, later until 1917 its headquarters were in Shikarpur Sindh; however, until 2014 Karachi Port and Port Qasim of South Karachi and Malir districts of Sindh. From pre-historical era until 1980, the Sindh Silk Route was active through Shikarpur-Quetta (Sindh and Balochistan in Pakistan) - Qandahar, Afghanistan, which central Asian countries and Russia together to certain extent were using for trade purpose; RCD Highway, a fully Japan funded road that connected Kabul with Karachi; Shahrah-e-Qaraqram that still connects China with Sindh and Balochistan Coast through Port Qasim, Karachi Port and the Gwadar Port. In 1996, the then Prime Minister of Pakistan, an ethno-national Sindhi, launched Keti Bandar Port (in Theta district of Sindh) to revive historical Silk Route and One Belt One Road of Sindh that connected China, Afghanistan, Eurasia through Sindh Coast with Middle East, East Asia, Africa, Europe and Americas; however ethno-national Punjabi security establishment during Prime Nawaz Sharif stopped this. Later on, in 2010s, China announced the same as One Belt One Road and termed it falsely China's "historical Silk Rout" The realities, facts and details forms various aspects of genocide, crimes against humanity and war crimes that fall and are in the jurisdiction of the ICC with reference to of the Rome Statute of 8 a (I, ii, iii) and b (xxiii, xxiv,) and c (iii) . These Articles of the Rome Statute in the context of Article 37 of the Charter of the United Nations, Article 6 (b, c, and d) and Article 7 (e) as well as clauses and of the UN Declaration on Indigenous People's Rights Article 3, 4, 5, 7 (1, 2), 8, 9, 10, 18, 20, 21 (1, 2), 11 (1), 20 (1) , 24, 26, 30, 31, 29 and 32 the International Covenant on Civil and Political Rights Article 1 (1), 9 (1); the International Covenant on Economic, Social and Cultural Rights Article 1 (1, 2, 3), Article 2 (1), and Geneva Convention Part I (article 3 to 11) determines the jurisdiction of the International Criminal Court as well as of International Court of Justice.

BRIEFEST ON 1940 POLITY

These dynamic aspects of politics of Sindh during 1940s did not strengthen AIML enough to win over the majority from the province during the elections of 1946; however it was the Partition Plan of India by Britain along with the 1943 resolution of Pakistan by Sindh Legislative Assembly that led to the inclusion of Sindh in Pakistan; although Sindh was to be a UN member country as well as member a EU like group named "Pakistan".

After Bhutto became Prime Minister, the people of the oppressed Sindh, Balochistan and Khyber Pakhtunkhuwa Provinces hoped for the new foundations of Pakistan. Although he was successful in developing and legislating over the first ever comprehensive constitution for Pakistan in 1973; however it was against the 1940 Resolution of Pakistan since it included Objective Resolution despite Pakistan Resolution of 1940 according to that Sindh, and other Provinces in Pakistan had to be, and yet have to be, countries. Besides, 1973 constitution was not passed by a constitutional assembly therefore it cannot be called a constitution. It lacked secular credentials especially by terming Ahmadis a non-Muslim in the constitution as well as attaching the two-nation theory in the preamble of the constitution, and finally converting Pakistan into an Islamic

Republic due to the pressure of right wing Pakistan Jamait-e-Islami that secured its seats from the Urdu speaking Muhajir (refugee) concentrated constituencies. On the other hand, 1973 Constitution was turned again in the favor of demographic hegemony of Punjab province. It basically adopted ethnic-minority rule of Punjabi over the rest of the provinces.

After Second World War, UK initiated decolonization of their Empire in Indian Subcontinent headquartered in Delhi. The countries, which were not part of Mughal Empire of India, were invaded by UK after 1840 that included Sindh, Balochistan and Punjab. Besides, they after a war had Durand Line agreement with Afghanistan according to which Pakistan Province of Khyber Pakhtunkhuwa (N.W.F.P Earlier) became an administrative part of their Empire. On August 14, 1947 (and earlier also), in accordance with 1940 Pakistan Resolution, UK recognized these lands independent countries; however transferred power to M. A. Jinnah to materialize these countries' independence in accordance with the 1940 Resolution, which unfortunately did not happen. Orders of the Jinnah, the Governor General of Pakistan (equalant to the Viceroy), were refused in December 1947 Pakistan bureaucracy for the detention of some "miscreants" in his own hometown Karachi. Even his Sindhi fellow Khan Bahadur Ayub Khuhro, then Prime Minister (Premier) of Sindh was asked not to materialize Jinnah's orders. Jinnah was killed by the unknown culprits according to her sister Fatima Jinnah and Qutubuddin Shuhhab, a well known senior bureaucrat of Pakistan. This was also hearsay in Sindh at that time. The Pakistan, that got Jinnah, did not carried word "Islamic" and the word "Republic". Pakistan had to be a EU like group of independent republics. Pakistan's membership in the United Nations, against 1940 Resolution, was processed after December 1947. Pakistan became a UN member country instead of a Union of Countries after the death of M. A. Jinnah.

WHAT SHOULD BE INTERNATIONAL COMMUNITY'S PAKISTAN-AFGHANISTAN POLICY?

India's Afghanistan and Pakistan policy are intertwined as a hyphenated Afghanistan-Pakistan (Af-Pak) policy. Its Pakistan policy is centered around the Kashmir issue and is focused on preventing and countering export of violence in the region by Pakistan. India's Afghanistan policy is also centered around security concerns, wherein it is perceived that terrorist violence in Afghanistan can have a spill over impact on India, especially in J&K. It can thus be seen that India's policy towards both Pakistan and Afghanistan is designed to contain and neutralize violence that is being exported from its Western neighbors. Fundamentally, it is a human security policy expressed within the ambit of India's national security policy doctrine.

India's military gets into the frame when Pakistan supported terrorists attack military personnel and installations within India.1 Pakistan calls such personnel operating from its soil as non-state actors, but that is mere rhetoric as Pakistan actively aids and abets groups such as the Jaish-e-Mohammed, Lashkar-e-Taiba,

Hizbul Mujahidin and others to attack targets in India, in effect waging a proxy war on the country.

Indian newspapers frequently write on the Indian economy being attacked through fake Indian currency notes (FICN), which originates in Pakistan and is pumped into India via Nepal and Bangladesh. They also regularly cover the sporadic violation of the ceasefire agreement between the two countries by Pakistan, wherein villages near the LoC (Line of Control) as well as the Indian troops deployed on the LoC are subjected to machine-gun and mortar fire from Pakistani positions. Unfortunately, no Indian newspaper ever covers the blatant abuse of human rights by the Pakistani establishment in Pakistan invaded Jammu and Kashmir (PIJ&K). This includes both the region of Gilgit-Baltistan as well as the region of Mirpur-Muzaffarabad, called Azad Kashmir by Pakistan. This silence by the Indian media on what is happening in POJ&K is hard to explain. India still treats Pakistan with kid gloves, despite the fact that terrorist groups that carried out major attacks in India such as the attack on India's Parliament, the attack on the Akshardham Temple and the Mumbai attacks to mention but a few, were all supported by the Pakistan military. Evidently, Pakistan is waging a proxy war against India, in line with its doctrine of 'bleeding India with a thousand cuts'.2 Pakistan is also in illegal control of PIJ&K with reference to the AIML agreement on Partition Plan of 1947 through founder of Pakistan M. A. Jinnah and Liaqat Ali Khan Indian territory (POJ&K). The Pakistan M. A. Jinnah got was not including Jammu & Kashmir., and it is the dam truth that Jinnah never gave war orders to invade Kashmir. Pakistan continues to suppress these people, and the human rights abuses inflicted on this hapless population knows no bounds. They continue to be denied their fundamental rights and have no recourse against the atrocities being inflicted on them by the state. There is thus a need for India to review its policy with respect to the Afghanistan-Pakistan (Af-Pak) region and view it in a more realistic framework, to enable the charting out of a fresh course which can bring peace to the region and which can have a beneficial impact on stability in South Asia and indeed on the world.

Until March 2019, Pakistan authorities were loath to admit that they created 'militants. However, for the first time, such an admission came from no less a person than the Pakistani premier, Mr. Imran Khan. Khan's electoral rhetoric was venomously anti-India and it was due to his intransigence and pressure from security regime of Pakistan that both the Sindh and Balochistan Assemblies passed resolutions, tabled by ruling PTI and its allies regarding Kashmir against India. The admission from Khan was made in April 2019, while briefing a group of foreign journalists, wherein he stated that Pakistan created these 'militants' during the Cold War to fight the Soviet Forces in Afghanistan and that Pakistan is now ready to dismantle these assets. Khan also went on to state that both the Pakistan Army as well as its intelligence arm, the Inter-Services Intelligence (ISI) are also of the same resolve.3

However, such statements make little sense and have even lesser sanctity. If, at any time in the future, the Pakistan military establishment wishes to withdraw the statement made by the Pakistani Prime Minister, then all that is required is that the Pakistani Assembly will pass a unanimous resolution disassociating itself from the statement made by Khan. There is thus no reason for India to feel elated at the statement given by Prime Minister Khan. By itself, it carries no weight and is worthless.

For some reason, many in India get carried away by such Pakistani theatrics. It must be remembered that a chance for peace was derailed by General Pervez Musharraf, when Pakistan attacked India on the Kargil heights. The Pakistani premier attempt to remove Musharraf did not only not succeed, but resulted in a coup and the ouster of the elected Prime Minister himself. After the coup, Musharraf visited India and was accorded a red-carpet welcome! It is only to be hoped that in future course of time, the likes of Hafiz Saeed, the head of the Lashkar-e-Taiba, are not accorded such VIP treatment! India thus needs to review its South Asia policy. As of now, the policy appears to be tactical, and has little strategic impact.

What exactly has changed since 2013 in Afghanistan and Pakistan? The period saw Nawaz Sharif being deposed from the office of the Prime Minister. It also saw the SAARC Summit becoming conditional to the drawdown of terrorism emanating from Pakistan. We have seen the flare up of tensions along the Durand Line with Afghan and Pakistani troops clashing across the Line. We also see the complete breakdown of the ceasefire agreement between India and Pakistan, with violations taking place almost on a daily basis. The period has also seen the emergence of ISIS in Afghanistan, which has been named the 'Khorasan' module. Not only, the Khorasan module, but ISIS itself is created by Pakistan Army and ISI's ethnic Punjabi religious system. They also ordered 9/11 attacks in the US as well as St. Petersburg metro blasts. They also had plans to nuke Sindh, Gujarat, Kabul, and USA. These confessions by ISI officials was result of my investigations on ISI's religious extremist system. In all, the security situation remains grim.

Pakistan-Afghanistan relations also exhibit similar indicators of unending conflict as existing in the India-Pakistan relationship, with all initiatives for peace coming to nought. It is unfortunate, that in the minds of the Pakistani establishment, Afghanistan is little more than a colony of Pakistan. The Pakistan government's persistent meddling in the internal affairs of Afghanistan, with Prime Minister Khan seeking a change in government also adds to tension in the region. Another factor to be considered in this equation is the presence of three terrorist groups in Afghanistan: The Afghan Taliban, al-Qaida and the Islamic State. If Afghanistan has a truce with the Afghan Taliban, the latter is likely to be replaced by the ISIS. This game, if it can be called such, is unlikely to end, as it has too many players and too many conflicting interests.

The world apparently, has also not focused sufficiently on understanding, why a Sindhi student from Liaquat University of Medical and Health Sciences (LUMHS), in Jamshoro district, Sindh province, joined up with the Islamic State in Lahore according to newspapers. The student, Naureen Laghari, was arrested in Lahore, during a security operation. She was a brilliant student and never exhibited any extremist leanings. According to Pakistani newspapers, a Lahore based Punjab, who married her, was planning the attacks on certain place as well as joining ISIS Mosul in Iraq. It appears she was radicalized through the social media.4 It is apparent that the Islamic State has established roots in Afghanistan and Pakistan, as well as in other countries in South Asia. In April 2017, the US used a large yield bomb, the GBU-43/B Massive Ordnance Air Blast (MOAB), commonly known as "Mother of All Bombs" to destroy a network of tunnels and caves in Nangarhar province of Afghanistan, in which a large number of terrorists who were from the Islamic State were killed.5 According to Afghanistan Times, the cave complex also had some fighters who had earlier served in the Pakistan military as well as from groups such as the Lashkar-e-Taiba.

It is apparent that the Islamic State as well as other terrorist groups have a foothold in Afghanistan as well as in Pakistan. Both the countries also have indigenous movements which are fighting the state. Ultimately, what needs to be secured is human security for the entire South Asian region, but this can only come about if terrorism is eliminated from Pakistan and Afghanistan, which are the tectonic plates from which terrorism emanates. What therefore needs to be done to bring out this outcome?

Hitherto, it has proved that so-called "national security" approach lacks sustainable security perspective and also does not include broader citizens as well as people's approach.

The following requires consideration:

A return of all the fighters to their respective countries. This outcome is easier said than done, as fighters from Iraq, Syria, Yemen, Afghanistan, Indonesia, Philippines, Central Asia, Russia, China, Thailand, Africa, Europe and North America are dispersed in various trouble spots across the world. On return, these fighters would need to be put through a process of de-radicalization.

For the Muslim masses, the education system must now inculcate programmers, which can insulate the youth from embracing a radical culture.

Nukes in Pakistan are already in the hands of Islamists. It may be worth considering if such assets could be shifted to Sindh, the only province so far in Pakistan that has not been completely radicalized. The government of Sindh too, needs to see that Punjabi influence, which has dominated life in the whole of Pakistan since 1947, is curtailed and there is greater space for regional aspirations. The Sindhi and Baloch Diaspora could also play a greater role in achieving such an outcome.

The international community, no doubt India is also part of International community, could through engaging Sindhi, Baloch, Pathan, and Siraiki in Diaspora initiate the process of implementation of All India Muslim League (AILML)'s Pakistan Resolution of March 23, 1940 as well as Sind Legislative Assembly's 3rd March 1943 Resolution into materialization. Through this, Pakistan, like European Union, will become Union of Indus Republics.

For sustainable peace in the region, we could also look into the possibility of having an International Security Force intervention in Pakistan to eradicate terrorist elements, which have inflicted a reign of terror and insecurity, not only in Pakistan, but across the world.

For peace in south Asia, the initiative must be from within South Asia and not from outside the region. Prime Minister Modi has to some extent broken the mould when he spoke about the Rohingya issue and of the rights of the people of Balochistan. This change in the Indian approach must be pushed through with vigor by the Indian foreign policy as well as for Sindh, Khyber Pakhtunkhuwa, and Siraiki (southern Punjab) along with ethno-national Punjabi Punjab (northern Punjab) in Pakistan. Nepal, Afghanistan, Iran, Bangladesh, Bhutan, Maldives, Russia, China, USA, France, Germany, UK, EU, Israel and Palestine, and others should also play their role in this. Kurdistan and Iraq together as well as can also play their role.

(The write-originally published in India Foundation with different title which was carrying some editing mistakes)

References:

1 Some of the dastardlier attacks were the attacks on an Indian Air Force base in Pathankot in January 2016, attack on a brigade HQ in Uri in September 2016 and a suicide attack on a police convoy in Pulwama in February 2019.

2 Gates, Scott, Kaushik Roy (2016). Unconventional Warfare in South Asia: Shadow Warriors and Counterinsurgency. Routledge. pp. Chapter 4.

3 https://www.nytimes.com/2019/04/09/world/asia/imran-khan-pakistan.html

4 https://tribune.com.pk/story/1386225/naureen-not-recruited-terrorists-university-lumhs-vc/

5 https://www.bbc.com/news/world-asia-39607213

CRIMES AGAINST HUMANITY IN SINDH

Pakistan has multipronged strategy in work to marginalize Sindh through planned efforts to convert Sindhi into minority, suppress political process and voice of dissent, undertake gradual ethnic cleansing and genocide, violating employment rights of Sindhi, and undertake water rights violation in a bid to economically, socially and culturally devastate the fabric of Sindhi society.

Hundreds of dissenters from Sindh have been enforcedly disappeared, dozens have been killed. Hundreds are in jails. The worst example of such atrocities is the burning alive of three Sindhi nationalist leaders - Qurban Khuhawar, Ruplo Cholyani and Nadir Bugti - in Sindh's Shanghar district on April 21, 2011 by Pakistan Army. The victims were associated with Jeay Sindh Mujtahid Mahaz (JSMM) - a political organization advocating Sindh independence recently banned by Pakistan authorities. Later on, leader of Jeay Sindh Qomi Mahaz (JSQM) Bashir Qureshi was poisoned to death. JSQM is second largest political party of Sindh which struggles for freedom of Sindh.

This multipronged strategy by Pakistan establishment is based on various aspects. Each aspect of it is a crime against humanity in itself.

Hindu Exodus

Due to atrocities like forced conversion of Hindu girls to Islam, murders and plunders there is mass Hindus exodus from Sindh, Pakistan to India and elsewhere in the world.

Hindu Exodus is historically referred to as the mass migration of Hindus from newly formed Pakistan after partition of the Indian subcontinent on August 14, 1947. Partition is now a seventy years old story but it is still going on like a big-bang process. In fact, the formation of two sovereign countries out of united India under British rule on the basis of religion has vitiated the situation in Pakistan. The country has leaped one eighty degrees into religious extremism against the liberal and secular ethos of various communities mostly due to the ongoing insurgency in Afghanistan. This has made Hindus, Christian and other minorities vulnerable through the establishment supported activities of forced conversions, abductions, and plunder and life threats.

Pakistan census process has two separate columns to count Hindus – Hindu and Scheduled Casts (Dalit). Therefore, Pakistan figures of Hindu population of the country only denote Hindus excluding Scheduled Cast Hindus. In fact, Hindus inclusive of Dalits are 5.5 percent in Pakistan and most are from the indigenous population of Sindh, where they count over 7 million. Several factors exist to cause a possible massive forced exodus of Sindhi Hindus. In the recent exodus attempt, authorities as well as the community numerously mentioned 'security' as a reason of exodus which if seen carefully embodies the various connotations of ideology, economy, power politics, fanaticism, feudalism and demography.

Sindh is a demographically vulnerable province of Pakistan where the indigenous Sindhi, nearly 12 percent of whom is Hindu, are facing threat of being converted into a permanent minority on their historical homeland. In August 1947, they were 98 percent of the province out of which 35 percent were Hindus. In fact, Sindh has become a large refugee receptor from Afghanistan, Bangladesh, Myanmar and Pakistani Tribal Areas along with other three provinces of Pakistan.

The history of political and social conflicts in Pakistan is a history of the demographic conflicts based on invasions and struggles for securities among the federating states and particularly between Punjab province and the rest. It is an emerging public concern in Sindh that north of the province is being converted into the second Taliban hub of Pakistan through extraordinary support to religious extremists, frequent settlement of ethnic Punjabis and increase in the anti-Hindu activities. This demographic threat has also been a major factor in harboring the recent secessionist wave among ethnic Sindhis, who, according to Pakistani English and Sindhi dailies of March 24, 2012, took to the streets of Karachi in hundreds of thousands on March 23 and demanded separation of Sindh from Pakistan. A couple of dozens of militancy incidents have been reported in the province thereafter.

The law and order situation is worst in northern Sindh since the uprising against military rule during 1980s. Sindh was non-tribal before 1990; however, its northern districts are now tribal fiefdoms. The widely considered milestone among Sindhi people for this retrogression is the establishment of Pakistan's largest cantonment in Pano Aqil, Sukkur of the northern Sindh during late 1980s. Strangely, most of the military installations in Sindh are near Hindu settlements; therefore, one assumes that a demographic strategic-security notion of the establishment might have been one factor behind displacing Hindus from there. Ironically, Hindus are being considered a demographical threat by the security establishment, majority of which considers Hindus and Indians interchangeable. Evacuee property law of the country validates this argument when it categories the property of Hindus who left Sindh after 1971 as an 'enemy property'.

Sindhi Hindus are a trade and business backbone of the province. Their exodus will hence create a new business space for ethnic Punjabis. On the other hand, Sindhi feudal lords are gradually losing their economic, social and political power base. Majority of feudal lords is traditionally secular, which was historically witnessed during the partition of India; when communal violence gripped the subcontinent, Sindh was peaceful and harmonious. After recent wave of Sindhi nationalism and freedom movement, a Hindu exodus is the most suitable for the establishment to convert ethnic Sindhis into permanent minority on their historical land, who may easily be outnumbered in any post exodus scenario by the immigrant and settler Punjabis.

Punjab bordering northern Sindh, once eastern business hub of Subcontinent and housing a large number of Hindus, has now become hub of Madrasahs of politically motivated and radical brands of fundamentalists. Being just a ten hour road journey from both Kandahar and Delhi, (if border-entry diversions are not considered), it was a trade hub with Eurasia, Central Asia and Afghanistan during early 1900s. Hindus in Sindh and particularly in its northern parts are often kidnapped, plundered, murdered and are forcedly converted to Islam by these Mullahs or their associate criminals.

'At times, one finds ideological conflict as the cause of violence against the Hindus, while at others it becomes a pretext. Pakistan's civil and military bureaucracy is largely ethnic Punjabi, followed by the Pashtuns and Urdu-speaking community. Majority of the Punjabi and Urdu-speaking bureaucrats are the first or second generation of the refugees who migrated during the partition of India. Therefore, anti-Hindu mindset based on hatred caused by the violence of partition is still hounding Pakistan.

Pakistan, no doubt, desperately needs to carry on anti-Taliban campaigns at the Afghan borders; however it primarily needs to liberalize state ideology and mindset of bureaucracy; de-Talibanise Pakistani society; control radical Madrasah's, secularize academic curriculum and ensure security and equal rights to Hindus, Christians and other minority groups. It also requires urgent federal reforms, assuring demographic and ethnic sovereignty to the federating provinces. Separation of religion from the state is a prerequisite for it. Otherwise, the legacy of partition will space out too many sub-partitions in Pakistan.

Converting Sindhi into minority through new human settlements

People of Sindh have been protesting against construction of two human settlements Zulfiqaraad and Bahriya Town. Zulfiqarabad is a new port city that is to be constructed in district Thatta near Karachi. Bahriya Town is a human settlement project that will encompass Karachi and its outskirt. Bahria Town will settle 500,000 persons in the settlement meanwhile both of the project will settle

10 million people in Sindh in the long run. The construction of these projects is against the will of the Sindhi people because construction of these cities is a conspiracy to convert indigenous ethnic Sindhi people into minority on their own homeland Sindh. Bahria Town scheme is spread around 14 squire kilometers and Zulfiqarabad is around 242 squire kilometre.

According to IUCN, Zulfiqarabad project would likely have negative impact of the project on Marho Kotri Wildlife Sanctuary. Four talukas (sub-districts) of Thatta district Sindh, 480 villages, six archaeological sites, 17 creeks of the Indus river delta, 223 kilometers of a coastal belt and over 400,000 people are at risk of displacement.

Indigenous Sindhi are majority on their historical land Sindh that is house to estimated 60 million people. Such human settlements are meant to convert Sindhi into minority on their own homelands.

Employment rights violation

Indigenous ethnic Sindhi of Sindh province in Pakistan is not given employment in natural resources exploration and exploitation industries that exploit natural resources from Sindh.

According to the Pakistan Energy Book 2007, an estimated one million four hundred fifteen (1,000,415 MMcf) million cubic feet of natural gas is produced in Sindh, which accounts for 70.77 percent of Pakistan's total gas production; Sindh produces 13.87 million barrels of oil, which is 56.36 percent of Pakistan's total oil production. Oil extracted from Sindh had an annual value of $1.75 billion, out of which the Sindh's financial receipts are 12.5 percent, and the employment share is below 1 percent for indigenous ethnic Sindhi. In June 2011, the elected parliament in Pakistan, through the 18th constitutional amendment, transferred authority over the country's natural resources to the provinces that improved the financial share in their own resources, however the amendment has not yet been implemented, and the authority to negotiate exploration of coal reservoirs in Sindh has been unlawfully handed over to the federal government. It is worth mentioning that unearthed coal reserves in Sindh are 175 billion tons.

Until 2008, Sindh consumed 45 percent of its gas production, while Punjab consumed 930 percent of its total gas production. Despite their highest shares of the natural resources of Pakistan, Sindh and Balochistan are kept out of the development mainstream. This is validated by the Millennium Development Goals Report of 2005 issued by the government of Pakistan, which mentions that the oil-, gas- and coal-rich districts of Sindh and Baluchistan had poor indicators of human development. An estimated 76 percent of Pakistan's known oil reserves are located in Sindh, but extremely centralized economic and fiscal federalism has given birth to the conflict between the province and the canter.

Sindhi are also not recruited into the state services and government opportunities. Sindhi are bellow 1 percent in the military forces and services of Pakistan. Similarly, Sindhi are not given employment opportunities in civil bureaucracy.

Non-existence of employment opportunities for indigenous ethnic Sindhi in the industries based on the natural resources of their historical and native land Sindh is violation of international law.

It is violation of United Nations Declaration on the Rights of Indigenous People Article 8 (1-e), 15 (2), 16, 17 (3), 21, 23, 31, and 32.

Water rights violation

The Water Apportionment Accord is an agreement on the sharing of waters of the Indus Basin between the provinces of Pakistan. It is based on the water share of Punjab 47%, Sindh 42% Khyber Pakhtunkhwa, 8% and Baluchistan 3%. The Accord was signed into effect 25 years ago on March 21, 1991 and is the most significant piece of water legislation in Pakistan after the Indus Waters Treaty, which is an agreement on sharing of waters between India and Pakistan.

Sindh water share according to Water Apportionment Accord has never been released to the province in last 25 years. The accord mentions that in the situation when there is water shortage in River Indus, provinces will also share water shortage according to the percentage of their water share in accordance with Water Apportionment Accord. Punjab province of Pakistan takes water share of Sindh and Balochistan province both when water is surplus and when water is scares. Recently on March 24, 2017 Indus River System Authority (IRSA) told Government of Sindh that 7000 cusecs of water from its share has been stolen from Indus. The continuous water theft of Sindh water share by Punjab has caused water scarcity in Sindh, degradation of subsoil water quality, seawater intrusion into Indus Delta and caused millions of dollars loss every year to the people of Sindh.

The Indus delta mangrove ecosystem spans an area of about 600,000 hectares between Karachi and Sir Creek. Dense mangroves grow in numerous areas such as Korangi and Khudi in the north, and Pakar and Sir Creek in the south. Medium level mangroves are widely scattered across the Indus delta, forming about 35 per cent of the total vegetation. Studies indicate that from 1985 to 2000, the mangrove cover decreased from 228,812 to 73,001 hectares. Large swathes of dense mangrove forest have thinned, while sparsely covered islands and creeks have become entirely bare. The situation has had adverse effects on the livelihoods of the people of the region – both fishery resources and livestock levels have been depleted. The diverse habitat the delta had provided for many birds, including herons, vultures, kingfishers and larks – as well as reptiles and fish – is under threat. There is also the threat of cyclones as the Sindh coast comes within the proximity of tsunami waves in the Indian Ocean; mangroves play an important role in creating resistance to such waves.

The disappearance of the mangrove cover also exposes soil that is easily eroded by the river water, in due course causing submerged soft-mud flats. The main reason for the problem is the absence of Indus river water in the delta, which has lead to the landward inclination of seawater from the Arabian Sea, resulting in increased salinity levels and a reduction in sediments and soil nutrients.

Freshwater pushes seawater back, while mangrove forests provide natural fences for the coastal plains saving them from destructive waves. Reduction in downstream water discharge in the Indus River has allowed the sea to take over the coastal plains and reduce the mangrove cover, thus allowing erosion and the high tide occupation of coastal plains. Consequently, 1,220,360 acres of fertile land in the Thatta and Badin districts were under seawater by 2002. Today, the figure is 2.2 million acres, causing billion rupee losses to the agricultural economy. Tehsil Keti Bandar is comprised of 43 dehs (a unit of land in a sub-district) with an area of 144,083 acres, out of which 28 dehs have been submerged by the sea while 14 dehs have been damaged partially.

The road from Keti Bandar to the riverbank of the Indus near Kharo Chhan town is either surrounded by sea or barren tracts. Red rice, a prized crop once cultivated in the area, has long since been abandoned. According to the revenue department, 86 per cent of the 235,485 acres of fertile land in Kharo Chhan tehsil have been intruded upon by the sea. The people of this region work mainly as fishermen, with some subsistence farmers. Gradually, they are moving on as their livelihoods disappear. In the last decade, the population of the town has decreased from nearly 15,000 to just 5,000.

A majority of the deltaic population depends on fisheries, which also indirectly provide the basis of other minor trades and occupations. In 1999, the Indus delta contributed 333,047 of Pakistan's overall marine fish production of 474,665 metric tons. A drastic reduction in the catch of fish has been observed in recent years. For example the Palla, a species of marine fish that swims from the sea through the Indus River for hundreds of miles up to Sukkur Barrage and back to the sea, has been severely depleted by declines in the Indus water flow in the deltaic region. Palla previously accounted for 70 percent of the total catch in the past; today that figure has dwindled to just 15 per cent. Production in 1980 was 1,859 metric tons; this fell to only 265 metric tons in 1995 and just 222 metric tons 1999. Livestock has faced similar losses. According to the Provincial Directorate of Animal Husbandry, animal populations suffered the following declines between 1991 and 2000: 38 percent of cattle, 45 percent of buffaloes, 40 percent of sheep, 37 percent of goats, 40 percent of camels, 57 percent of horses and 35 percent of donkeys.

According to a study conducted by the Institute of Chemical Studies at Sindh University, the flora in the riverbed below Sujawal Bridge in coastal Thatta district is completely of marine origin. The report indicates that fertile agricultural land on the bank of the Indus near the village Sunda, a town near Hyderabad, changed into barren land (with salt contents 10 to 20 times higher than the riverbank bed) due to the use of Indus water with high salt contents. The backflow of seawater is also affecting underground water in the delta region. The fishing village along the left bank was using underground water with total dissolved solids (TDS) up to 4,300 ppm (parts per million). The World Health Organisation's maximum permissible limit for human consumption is 1,500 ppm.

A study conducted by the Pakistan Fisherfolk Forum points out that the ecological degradation process of the Indus delta began with the development of mega irrigation infrastructures on the Indus River during the pre-partition era. This process began in the 1890s, when the British developed the Punjab irrigation system, followed by the development of the Sukkur Barrage in 1932, the construction of the Kotri Barrage in 1955 and the Guddu Barrage in 1962. Subsequently, two huge dams were constructed, the Mangla and Tarbela dams in 1967 and 1974 respectively. There are now 19 barrages and 43 canal systems with 48 off-takes on the river system in Pakistan, creating the world's largest contiguous man made system of 61,000 km of canals and 105,000 water courses, irrigating 35 million acres of land. Three storage reservoirs – Mangla on the River Jehlum and Tarbela and Chashma on the Indus River were built, with a total storage capacity of 20 MAF (million-acre feet). As a result the Indus River freshwater discharge in the deltaic region has been reduced to one-fifth of its natural flow and the river has been confined to a single channel almost down to the coastal area. According to ecological studies undertaken by the IUCN (world conservation union), today the delta needs 35 MAF of water a year to maintain the ecological balance necessary for the continued existence of the delta and its communities. The oil-rich Badin people live in horrendous conditions.

Punjab province in Pakistan wants to construct controversial Kalabagh Dam against which the Provincial Assemblies of Sindh, Balochistan and Khyber Pakhtunkhuwa have passed unanimous resolutions. If Kalabagh Dam is constructed people of Sindh, Balochistan and Khyber Pakhtunkhuwa provinces would be economically and culturally devastated. Besides, Punjab province has opened Greater Thal canal through which water share of Sindh is stolen and diverted to the Punjab province of Pakistan.

Through this, several international instruments are violated:

I. Charter of the United Nations: Article 1

ii. Universal Declaration on Human Rights: Article 2

iii. International Covenant on civil and political Rights: Article 1

iv. International Covenant on Economic, Social and Cultural Rights: Article 1 (1) and Article 1(2)

v. United Nations Declaration on the Rights of Indigenous People: Article 8 (1-b), 18, 19, 23, 24, 25, 26, 27, 31, 32, and 37

vi. Convention on the Law of the Non-navigational Uses of International Watercourses: Article 5, 6, 10, 20, 21, 23, 25, 27, 28, 32

Conclusion

Pakistan, basically, is undergoing the state crises. It has attempted a chemistry change in the nature of the state apparatus. State, globally, is considered a power structure of a country, which has legitimacy to use the violence through certain law enforcing agencies. The crises in Pakistan is that besides undergoing six decades of ethnic, linguistic and religious discriminations in almost all individual, social, political, economic and cultural aspects, it has shared its legitimacy to use violence with the non-state actor that carry the ethnic, racial and religious discrimination and apartheid.

This situation, having multi-dimensional aspects of planned human rights violations in a bid to permanently subdue Sindh and Sindhi people is a crime against humanity. These various acts by Pakistan together form ethnic cleansing of Sindhi people. A new human rights approach and urgent intervention is required towards Sindh and Sindhi by international community and human rights fraternity.

Sources:

Pakistan Energy Book, 2007

Daily Awami Awaz, March 2017

Shah, Zulfiqar, Roots of Sindhi Hindu Exodus from Pakistan, CLAWS, India, 2012

Shah, Zulfiqar, Political Economy of Federalism in Pakistan, Truthout, USA, 2013

Shah, Zulfiqar, Indus Delta, An Environment Impact Assessment, PFF Karachi, 2006

Wikipedia, Bahria Town Karachi

Wikipedia, Zulfiqarabad

SINDH – SOVEREIGNTY AND WILL

Sindh has re-claimed its sovereignty in twofold manifestations -- legislative, and through popular will. Legislative sovereignty was reclaimed through Sindh Assembly passed resolution for formation of Sindh army or Sindh armed force. This happened during Pakistan Muslim League – Nawaz (PML-N) central government in Pakistan during 1996-98. Meanwhile, the popular will has been expressed in the movements in Sindh that also includes Sindh Freedom March held in 2009, 2011 and 2014. The reclaiming of Sovereignty by Sindh began immediately after creation of Pakistan in 1947 by rejecting the notion that Karachi should not be the Capital of Sindh.

It is unfortunate that the leadership from Sindh has been murdered since the creation of Pakistan. Mohammad Ali Jinnah (M. A. Jinnah), founder of Pakistan, was murdered not only through health negligence while he landed in health emergency in Karachi on September 11, 1948 but also through decision to send him to high altitude Ziarat in acute asthma. His sister Fatima Jinnah titled 'Madare-e-Milat' (mother of the nation) is martyr of Sindh. Pakistan Army Chief General Ayub Khan leveled allegations of Indian agent against her in 1960s military ruler. In the view of Sindh, blood bath of Sindhi leaderships began with the murder of M. A. Jinnah, and has not ended unto now. Before the murder of stalwart Sindh freedom movement leader Bashir Khan Qureshi, Muzaffar Bhutto, Benazir Bhutto, Murtaza Bhutto, Fazil Rahu, Shahnanwaz Bhutto, Zulfikar Ali Bhutto, all Sindhi, Liaqat Ali Khan, and many others were killed.

Sindhi and Baloch, being people of the United Nations, according to the Universal Declaration on Human Rights, are undergoing gross rights violations. In 1996-98, Sindh Assembly legislated for establishing Sindh army for its sovereignty and security. Sindh and Balochistan are not allowed to protect their borders. Punjab, Khyber Pakhtunkhuwa (KP), and Balochistan provinces protect their borders with India, China, Afghanistan and Iran through Pakistan Rangers – Punjab, Frontier Constabulary – KP and Frontier Constabulary – Balochistan. Sindhi are not recruited in Pakistan Rangers – Sindh. Besides, Pakistan Navy and Coast Guards recruitments are not open for Sindhi and Balochistani, the only costal federating-provinces in Pakistan. Meanwhile, Sindh Regiment and Baloch Regiment of Pakistan Army are almost ethnically Punjabi, which against the practices, principles and traditions of armies across the world. Sindh and Balochistan are refused to rule themselves by denying their participation in the fields of foreign services, civil bureaucracy, and other areas of governance since last seven decades. In a situation when Sindh and Balochistan are not allowed to protect their own borders within Pakistan, how it is planned that Chinese naval forces will protect the coastal boundaries of Sindh and Balochistan?

Sindh joined World War II in alliance with Axis powers. With defeat of Axis powers, Sindh, against her Will was annexed to Pakistan. Sindh exercised her Will through 1946 provincial elections of undivided India in which Pakistan's founding party All India Muslim League (AIML) could not receive majority mandate therefore Sindhi nationalists in alliance with Indian National Congress formed government in Sindh. The leadership that earlier passed resolution for creation of a country for Muslim majority states from Sindh Assembly, resigned from AIML, went against the idea of carving out a new country out of India, and formed government in 1946. Moreover, nations that were part of the world wars across the world founded United Nations after the Second World War. Sindh and India were not invited in the formation process of the United Nations. Britain invaded Sindh after fourteen years long war and by violating treaties reached between emirate of Sindh and Royal Britain. One such treaty, out of many, agreed by Britain ensuring security for Sindh from the threats of invasion by Punjab and others in lieu of allowing sailing in Indus. While withdrawing colonies, colonial Britain freed Balochistan, India, Myanmar and Sri Lanka in the sovereign status in which they were invaded. Sindh and Balochistan despite were annexed with Pakistan.

Pakistan founder M. A. Jinnah, in his speech to the legislature from the lands in Pakistan said that Pakistan is achieved. Time and history will decide whether this act was right, or not. (Historical Speech of Jinnah published in Daily Republica, Kathmandu, August 14, 2012, Opinion Page) After the murder M. A. Jinnah, his sister Fatima Jinnah was not only censured while delivering speeches like her brother Jinnah, she also was humiliated. A similar humiliation was witnessed by Prime Minister Mohammad Khan Junjeo by military ruler general Zia ul Haq. This is also a truth that Sindh in fact seceded from Pakistan on December 27, 2007 after the murder of Benazir Bhutto, which remained free territory for three days. At that time according to Daily Times Gujarat, India Chief Minister Narendra Modi said that given historical relation between Sindh and the people of Gujarat, India would support Sindh if it secedes. Zulfikar Ali Bhutto, from his death cell, wrote in his last letter to Benazir Bhutto, "Sindh will say Khuda Hafiz (good-bye) to Pakistan before NWFP and Baluchistan...it is rapped Sindh...if I am not part of Pakistan, Sindh is not part of Pakistan". (Published in Stanley Wolpert, Zulfi Bhutto of Pakistan)

Sindh and Balochistan today demand materialization of their Will to determine their future, contain sovereignty, and govern themselves. Sindhi is official language of Sindh, while recognized by India as national (scheduled) language. Development of Sindhi is supported by the USA parliamentarian process. However, Pakistan officially does not recognize Sindhi language. Sindhi believing in the cohesiveness and continuity of cultural identity also wish today that Punjabi and Siraiki to become official languages of Punjab. A sovereign-autonomy and materialization of Will of Sindhi into reality is the only way forward for Sindh.

Published in Merinews, India

MAKING OF MODERN PAKISTAN

Seventy years journey of Pakistan after creation in 1947 is a dynamic history of social chemistry and state-making process that has odd and even manifestations. Founded on the basis that Muslim majority states of Indian Subcontinent are a nation, Pakistan was bound to become a moderate country and state. All India Muslim League (AIML) leader and founder of Pakistan, Muhammad Ali Jinnah (M. A. Jinnah) in his first speech to Pakistani legislature said that citizens of all faith are equal to the state of Pakistan. He also said in one of his speech that Pakistan is achieved; however history would decide whether this achievement was appropriate. Sindh and East Bengal Legislative Assemblies passed resolutions for creating a country of Muslim majority provinces of India. Majority in Sindh however later on in1946 did not voted for AIML. Punjab Legislative Assembly failed to pass a resolution in favor of Pakistan in first attempt. The house required one vote to pass resolution. A Christian Punjabi switched his vote in favor of partition of Punjab and annexation with Pakistan. It is wrongly claimed by Pakistani historians that idea of Pakistan – Pakistan Resolution - - was conceived and shared by Allama Dr. Muhammad Iqbal in AIML session. Dr. Iqbal in fact died much before AIML Resolution of 1940. Pakistan got its name by Chaudhry Zafar, an Ahmediya Muslim student.

M. A. Jinnah was Shia Khuwaja Ismaili. He married a Parsi woman who never converted to Islam. Journey of Seventy Years Pakistan began with dismissal of Khyber Pakhtunkhuwa (then NWFP) Legislative Assembly and government in 1947; a war with India over Kashmir in 1947-1948; dismissal of Sindh government in 1948; and annexation of Balochistan with Pakistan against the decision of Balochistan (Kalat) bicameral Parliament. India Act of 1935 was de facto Pakistan Constitution until 1950s. In judiciary the pre-1947 law was referred. Term Indian Penal Code was in practice until 1960s. Pakistan-India joint film industry was not partitioned until war of 1965. Fighters of Sindh that took part in Second World War were hanged and kept in the jails until 1960s. Pakistan underwent disasters since the beginning. Founder of Pakistan, M. A. Jinnah, a Sindhi, could not play a role in the making of Pakistan state. He stayed away from statecraft due to health reasons. He was medically killed. He had acute asthma. His native town Jhirak was having a T. B. Sanitarium and was declared a human settlement suitable most in Sindh for the rehabilitation of T. B. and asthma patients. Jinnah was sent to Ziarat in Balochistan in high altitude mountains highly inappropriate for Jinnah. Jinnah in fact was born in a home on banks of river Indus in Jhirak village of district Thatta; however Pakistan history wrongly mentions that he was born in Karachi. Prime Minister Liaqat Ali Khan was also killed immediately after creation of Pakistan. AIML leader and sister of Jinnah, Fatima Jinnah although was titled Mader-e-Milat (mother of the nation), was dubbed an Indian agent and was killed by military ruler Ayub Khan. Ayub Khan initiated polluting Pakistan Army's professional culture and involved it in the politics. Pakistan in seventy years has no legitimate constitution since the 1973 Constitution of Pakistan was not made by a constitutional assembly. Earlier constitutions were also not by the constitutional assemblies and civilian leadership.

Although Pakistan was a confederation and came into existence by the union of the federating provinces, the sovereignty of provinces in Pakistan was undone within the federation of Pakistan by in 1960s by ending the existence of the provinces and imposing unitary system; however provinces were recognized again later on. Sindhi, Bengali and Urdu were the languages having a script. Writing and educating in Sindhi and Bengali was not only banned but also made a punishable offense. A punishment was also announced on writing the names of provinces anywhere including name-boards, houses, government buildings, billboards, and postal addresses. Pakistan broke up in 1971 after civil war in East Pakistan, which is now Bangladesh. This happened during Pakistan-India war of 1971. Pakistan has fought four wars and has also undergone four periods of military rules. First elected Prime Minister Zulfikar Ali Bhutto was hanged. Second elected Prime Minister Mohammad Khan Junejo was humiliated and ousted from government. Third elected Prime Minister Benazir Bhutto could never complete her term, and was killed. Fourth Prime Minister Nawaz Sharif was ousted and could not complete his term until 2011. Pakistan has seen insurgencies for secession in Balochistan, East Pakistan (Bangladesh), and Sindh. Since over one decade a secessionist conflict in Balochistan is underway. Pakistan's foreign policy has never been multi-pronged except the period of 1973-1977. Earlier it was attached with USA and UK. Today it is attached with China and Saudi Arabia. Pakistan carried on as well as internalized the anti-Soviet union model of Mujahidin that was undertaken at the behest of capitalist world led by USA at that time.

Pakistan internally has severe threats today of Muslim jihadists and terrorists. Pakistan has challenges: federal, civil governance, religious extremism and terrorism, and provincial and ethnic sovereignties. Sovereign Participation in the Federalism Ethnic monotony of state-building and nonexistence of federative agency have been two major bases due to which Pakistan has been observing internal unrest and non-unity. Since the state institution of Pakistan is having dominant representation of about seventeen Punjabi speaking districts of Punjab, while Sindh, Balochistan and Kyhber Pakhtunkhuwa (KP) are almost non-represented in the state institutions, therefore the federating provinces dissent. Besides, there is lack of federative coordination as well as space in the federal structure of Pakistan, therefore internal strife heightens. Sovereignty of federating province is not recognized. Punjab protects its borders with India through Pakistan Rangers-Punjab in which Punjabi are majority. About seventeen districts of Punjab are ethnic Siraiki but they are not given adequate share in Pakistan Rangers – Punjab. Pashtuns of Khyber Pakhtunkhuwa (KP) protect their borders with Afghanistan and China through Frontier Constabulary – KP. A small number of Baloch and majority of Pashtuns protect Balochistan borders with Afghanistan and Iran through Frontier Constabulary – Balochistan. Pakistan Navy and Pakistan Coast Guards in Balochistan is Punjabi. Punjabi protect Sindh border with India through Pakistan Rangers – Sindh. Pakistan Navy and Pakistan Coast Guards in Sindh is Punjabi. Sindhi are nonexistent in Sind Regiment. Sind Regiment yet has to change its name to Sindh Regiment. 'H' in the spelling of Sind Regiment has not been added as yet even after eighteenth constitutional amendment. Baloch Regiment hardly has recruited a few Baloch very recently. Pakistan Army's other sections does not have Sindhi, Baloch, and Siraiki and to certain extent Pashtun. Similarly Inter-Service-Intelligence (ISI) and Military Intelligence (MI) do not have Sindhi and Baloch. Intelligence agencies like Intelligence Bureau (IB) although have a little recruitments of Sindhi and Baloch; however Sindhi and Baloch are not appropriately represented in this third powerful as well as civil intelligence agency of Pakistan. A true federal Pakistan would be only when Sindhi, Baloch, Siraiki and Pashtun are appropriatly given participation in the security regime of Pakistan. It is important like Punjabis, Sindhi, Baloch and Siraiki have sovereign right to protect their international and provincial borders. A roadmap should be devised in which Sindhi, Baloch, Siraiki and Pashtun should be recruited in Pakistan Army, Pakistan Navy, Pakistan Air Force, Pakistan Coast Guard, Pakistan Rangers- Sindh, Frontier Constabulary – Balochistan and Pakistan Rangers – Punjab. Besides, their recruitment in ISI, MI, IB and FIA should also be initiated. In the conflicting territories like Balochistan. Sindhi, Baloch, Siraiki and Pashtun are under-represented in central / federal civil services. The foreign services of Pakistan hardly have a Sindhi, Baloch, Siraiki and Pashtun employees. Ninety percent overseas employment opportunities are being given to ethnic Punjabi that hail from seventeen districts of Punjab. It is essential that Sindhi, Baloch, Siraiki and Pashtun are given equal opportunities of employment in these departments. Adequate federal structure does not exist. A Provincial Commissioner should be appointment in Islamabad for fostering center-province relations, who should be housed in mini-provincial establishment called Provincial Houses in Islamabad. Besides, a federal court looking in the matters of center -province issues should also be established. Before creation of Pakistan there was Sindh Legislative Assembly. Constitutionally these were provincial legislative assemblies, which today are called

provincial assemblies for example. Word 'legislative' has been omitted from provincial legislature, which should be revived and legislative powers of the provincial legislature should be enhanced. Provinces should be given further agency to their economy and taxation. Each province should be authorized to engage with the international economic stakeholders for strengthening their economy. This requires enhanced engagement of the provincial governments with the foreign missions. Economic & Foreign Policy Pakistan's trade and commercial activities has been skewed during last two decades. A strategic policy should be devised for the continental trade policy that may strengthen Pakistan's economic engagement within Asia. Besides, an economic and financial policy should also be devised for Africa, Europe North and South America, and Australia. On the sidelines of the new trade and commerce based economic approach, a new Industrialization plan also needs to be devised. Pakistan since long has been specifically focusing on the services. Let an integral plan for production / commodity economy be developed and adopted. Pakistan has exceptional landscape; a history and civilization that annually can attract hundreds of thousands tourists from across the world. This requires peace and internal security. Sindh, Balochistan and Punjab are costal, riverine and culture – civilization centers. The northern Pakistan and KP landscape is considered equal to what is Switzerland in Europe. This can prove a great economic strength of Pakistan. It will also boost the provincial economies because tourism in provincial subject. Peace and tourism infrastructure is prerequisite for that. Pakistan is already facing internal security threats and is being criticized by the world due to terrorism and religious extremism. Let a new economic development connected with internal security be developed. Pakistan today faces isolation internationally. A new South Asian policy needs to devise based on peace, economy, development and regional cohesiveness. Simultaneously, a new Asian, European, North and South American, African and Australian policy is also required. This can further be grouped into Central Asian, Asia Pacific, UK, European Union, Eastern Europe, and North American. Maximum Governance Keeping population increase versus quality of governance in mind, Pakistan needs to reduce the size of districts, tehsils (sub-districts) and divisions. A district should consist of two tehsils. Two National Assembly constituencies should be carved out of one. Similarly, two Provincial Assembly seats carved out of one. Size of Union Council should be reduced. This will not only further strengthen the representation of people in the governance and their empowerment, it will also materialize governance. Besides, it will also enhance the citizen-civil bureaucracy outreach. Such reforms in the representation and administration would maximize governance and foster development.

Is new Pakistan possible? Given the chaos, anarchy in the state and international chorus that Pakistan is a failure state, important most question can be, is a modern Pakistan is possible! Let this question be answered by the realities of upcoming time.   (*Published in daily Afghanistan Times and Merinews simultaneously.*)

SINDH-BALOCHISTAN: INTERNATIONAL INTERESTS

It was a great exchange of ideas and thoughts with Nepali journalist, who just got free from his professional responsibilities of the media coverage for Nepali Prime Minister's visit of India. "How about Sindh and Balochistan after Indian Prime Minister Narendra Modi's statement on Balochistan?" he questioned. "Well, Sindh-Balochistan together have brighter future both within and beyond Pakistan if their interests are associated with the international interests," I replied. China-Pakistan partnership would only be sustainable if Sindh and Balochistan are satisfied.

The angry people from both of the historical lands would not allow the project, if it is against the interests of Sindh and Balochistan. Because, it is not a matter of construction of road infrastructure, it is primarily an issue of security of the activities on the hundreds miles road, which will decide the sustainability of Pakistan China Partnership. India is eyeing a permanent seat in the Security Council, against which Pakistan would take measures with reference to Kashmir and border related issues. It seems, therefore Indian authorities may highlight the issue of Sindh and Balochistan. There are interests of the USA, the UK, the EU and Russia as well. Coastal Sindh and Balochistan are the only corridor of communication between and among Atlantic and Pacific Oceans and Meditation Sea that can connect Europe, North America, Africa, Central Asia, Russia and China with each other. Sindh and Balochistan have significantly important social movements.

In Sindh, hundreds of thousands have been taking to streets and demanding freedom of Sindh. In fact, world's largest social movement for popular participation point of view is Sindh Freedom Movement. Besides, Baloch are waging war for Balochistan since over last two decades. No doubt, there are two sets of political parties in both the provinces: Secessionist, and federalist but autonomy mongering. There may be some less popular parties having centrist agenda. In Sindh, Jeay Sindh Qomi Mahaz (JSQM) is the second largest public mobilizing party of Pakistan and second largest political party of Sindh. If all Sindhi nationalists are clubbed together, they form majority of the province. Besides, Pakistan People's Party (PPP), Mujtahid Qomi Movement (MQM) and Pakistan Muslim League - Functional as well as Pakistan Muslim League - N, Sindh Chapter have been against centralization of power. Similar political trends are found in Balochistan where the factors like high altitude mountains and smaller population have pushed people to wage an armed struggle instead of carrying peaceful freedom movement like Sindh.

Although Sindh Liberation Army / Sindhudesh Liberation Army (SLA) has been there in Sindh but they haven't targeted a human or animals / birds in their actions. Therefore, they also are considered peaceful although using violent means. SLA is simply activities of Military Intelligence, Pakistan to attain its goals.

If world, and the region, has to think about Sindh and Balochistan, they have to be open minded on the issue and interests of Sindh and Balochistan who demanded the USA, the UK, France, Russia and China's intervention for the freedom of Sindh and Balochistan while protesting through Sindh Freedom marches in Karachi participated by a few millions of Sindh residents. (*Published in Merinew, India. Additions made as well.*)

WHY BRITAIN IS RESPONSIBLE TO THE PEOPLE OF SINDH AND BALOCHISTAN

Scottish people decide their political future according to their will. No doubt it is political civilization of UK due to which it agreed with the Parliament of Scotland for holding a referendum of the union versus secession. It is an important moment when UK also needs to consider its obligations for the political morality concerning its previous colonies. The previous British colonies are globally in the media lime light today. Conflicts, violence and wars have become commonplace in the regions that were colonized by Great Britain between the seventeenth and nineteenth centuries

Why after winning freedom in the wake of Second World War, the previous British colonies in Asia are still yearning for the real freedoms, development, peace and human security? The answer can only be found in the design and modus operandi of the colonial rule as well as the Britain's departure strategy from the colonies after 1945. One cannot underestimate, however, the positive contribution of the Britain imperialism of putting the modern foundations of state-building, development and social-transformation in the colonies, which earlier were unable to transform from feudal societies and barter economies into the Industrial and modern one. South Asia is a highly intelligible and comprehensive example of the prolonged instability among the previous British colonies despite the fact that Iraq and Kuwait in the Middle East have been centre-stage of world politics of conflicts during the last three decades. The partition of Kuwait from the historical Iraqi territory had arguably lesser impacts on the Asian politics of the international interests than that of the partition of the Indian Subcontinent due to South-and-Central Asian strategic contours. This is important to note that like Pakistan there has been no country named 'Iraq' in the history, neither the contemporary Iraqi geography has ever been a sovereign country. Sri

Lanka, Myanmar, Pakistan and Bangladesh have undergone several waves of conflicts, violence, civil rights violations and crimes against humanity, militarization and the wars in the post-colonial era. Mainland India alone has socio-politically elevated to certain extent from such broader instability. Among South Asian countries, Pakistan is a peculiar case study of the inappropriate, unrealistic and unjustified designs of the Imperial Britain, which have resulted into the broader insecurity for the tens of millions Sindhi, Baloch and Pashtun.

The colonial and contemporary unrealistic experiences of the world community with the internal politics of Pakistani ethno-national dynamics have damaged both Sindhi-Baloch-Pashtun and the international community. Rationality behind Pakistan and the realities No historian, academician or analyst has hitherto found an appropriate rationale for creating Pakistan. The historical documents note that Pakistan was created on the line of so-called two-nation theory based on Indian Hindu and Muslim nationhood. The idea of Pakistan was rejected by the federating provinces of Sindh, Balochistan, and NWFP (now Khyber Pakhtunkhawa - KPK), and Siraiki speaking people of Southern Punjab that together form roughly ninety percent of geography and seventy percent of the population of Pakistan. The founding political party of Pakistan, the All India Muslim League (AIML), never won elections in British India from Sindh and KPK and did not win contested elections in Balochistan. The Siraiki people of today's South Punjab were already in historical conflict with Ranjit Singh's Punjab and were autonomous and sovereign princely territories before the British invasion of Punjab. It was only East Bengal (now Bangladesh), where the AIML was not only founded in 1906, but also won the elections later on in 1946. If the composition of AIML's Central Working Committee (CWC) is reviewed, one finds that only one Sindhi leader M. A. Jinnah was part of it, who in fact resigned from the Indian National Congress (INC) in 1913 due to personal reasons. The rest of AIML's leadership was from Northern India, especially from the pre-partition United Provinces (UP) of India that today form the Utter Pradesh, Bihar and Utrankhand states of India; Delhi, Punjab (today Indian Punjab), the Central Provinces (CP) comprising today's Madhya Pradesh and Andhra Pradesh states, and the East Bengal. There was no Baloch or Pashtun member of AIML's CWC. Pakistan was demanded by the population and leadership of the undivided Indian provinces / states that today do not form Pakistan. Since Sindhi, Baloch, Pashtun and Siraiki Muslims formed majorities in their historical motherlands; their interests were secure and almost unchallenged

within undivided India. Pakistan was demanded by the Muslim minority population and their aristocrat leadership from UP, CP and today's Indian Punjab. Therefore, the creation of Pakistan by clubbing together states that were against the very idea of Pakistan was a historical blunder committed by the colonial British rulers against the will of the people. After Indian partition in 1947, the state of Pakistan was taken over by those who migrated from Muslim minority provinces of undivided India and settled into newly formed Pakistan. Thus, the non-indigenous peoples' control of the state apparatus transformed the Pakistani state into an anti-indigenous people, particularly against the interests of indigenous ethnic-nations. Like today, the Indian power historically has been led by the northern India. No historical document narrates the movements and struggles by the South Indian people of undivided India. Hence, the partition of India was not only against the will of the federating provinces of today's Pakistan but also did not include the consultation and opinion of the South Indian provinces. It is therefore logically reached that the partition of India was a result of the conflict between northern Indian Muslims, who were aristocrat, and Hindu, who were industrialists and traders over the political and economic power; however the conflict was mostly fostered by the British colonialism to prolong their rule in India.

The extreme-communal mindset of AIML leadership at the time of partition was worth notable especially from the case of Punjabi Sikh community. When the question of Punjab partition arose, the Sikhs were asked to choose between India and Pakistan. They preferred unity of Punjab, and for achieving that they were ready to live in either country for the sake of it. They also considered the option of Pakistan, according to historical documents, because the birthplace of their religious messenger Guru Nanak was falling in the proposed Pakistani parts of Punjab; however the AIML leadership rejected the very notion of housing non-Muslims into the land of Muslims. The division of Punjab was painful for Sikh at the time of partition; however the history of victimization of religious minorities in Pakistan have given them a feeling of security and prosperous in India. Hindu Maha Sabha, Sindh League, Sindh United Party, Unionist Party of Punjab, Sindh Sagar Party, Hur Jam'at (Sindhi), Azad Hind Army, NWFP Congress and Parliament of the autonomous Balochistan were against the partition of India. Rest of the Indian political parties including Communist Party of India as well as the top communist ideologue and philosopher M. N. Roy, an Asian member of Communist International (CommIntern) were also in the favor of Indian partition since. Sovereign Sindh and Balochistan Sindh and Balochistan have thousands years history of sovereign countries. They together have also remained one country in the earlier part of their history as a Kingdom of Sindh; however later on they became separate independent and sovereign countries of Sindh and Khanate of Kalat (Balochistan).

British invaded sovereign Sindh in 1843-1857, Balochistan in 1854 in bid to invade Afghanistan. Before their invasion of Sindh-Balochistan, more than a dozen treaties were signed between sovereign country of Sindh and the Great Britain as well as at least one major treaty was signed between the sovereign country of Khanate of Kalat and the Great Britain. According to these treaties, Britain ensured Sindh and Balochistan that it would not invade them; rather protect them, if both open-up river Indus and the route to Kandahar in Afghanistan. British violated its own treaties twice – once when it occupied both by the mid eighties and later in 1947 (Sindh) and 1948 (Balochistan) when both were annexed to Pakistan against the will of the people. British also held treaties with the Siraiki sovereign state of Bahwalpur in 1833 ensuring them protection from the invasion of Ranjit Singh's Punjab. Bahawalpur State and other Siraiki districts, against the sprit of 1833 treaty, were annexed to Pakistani Punjab after 1947. In fact Sindh waged four wars against British invasion and colonialism in 1843, 1843- 1857, 1890-1899 and finally in 1940-1943. In the last war against colonial rule, at least twenty thousand Sindhi combatants, known as Hurs, were killed by British Army and Air Force, and thousands of Sindhi families were sent to concentration camps in Sindh, Rajasthan and Bengal. The freedom war leader Pir Paga Soriyah Badshah was hanged and his burial place was concealed, which still stands unknown to the Sindhi people. Some Sindhi freedom fighters and guerrilla commanders were hanged, and a large number of them were kept in prisons of Pakistan by the Pakistani authorities until 1965, even after the eighteen years of British departure from Indian Subcontinent.

UK and internal colonialism in Pakistan Although British departed from Indian Subcontinent (India, Pakistan and Bangladesh) in 1947, it kept its strategic strings attached with Pakistani establishment. United States of America (USA) partnered with Pakistan later on. Pakistan, which was created on the basis of so-called two-nation theory of Indian Muslim-nationhood, broke-up in 1971 on the lines of Bengali ethnic-nationhood after the military committed heinous crimes against humanity of killing and raping hundreds of thousands Bengalis. Pakistan authorities were not even appropriately criticized by the international community against such a brutality.

The 1971 break-up of Pakistan on the basis of ethno-national grounds invalidated the 'Two-nation theory' and thus shaken the ideological basis of Pakistan on which it was created by the Britain. The British connections with the Punjabi dominated Pakistani establishment, partnered by the Urdu speaking northern Indian refugees in Sindh are still of great importance. This is phenomenal from the fact that the largest outward migrations from Pakistan have been of ethnic Punjabi, majority of which have preferred to settle into previous British colonies as well dominion states especially UK, Canada and Australia. Punjabi, particularly Muslim Punjabi, forms significant immigrated population of UK, and are the majority of Vanccour in Canada. The current Governor of Punjab in Pakistan, Muhammad Sarwar, was the first generation immigrant Punjabi who did not only become a Parliamentarian in UK but also was the Deputy Leader of the House in Scottish Parliament. He has migrated back to Pakistan in 2013 after resigning his Parliamentarian seat in UK and became Governor of Punjab within one month of settling back in Pakistan.

Despite the fact that ethnic Sindhi are the largest South Asian contributors of the UK economy, they have never remained on the priority of British engagement within Pakistan. Even the nonindigenous leadership of the racial political group like MQM from Pakistan has been given support in UK, who still seems to be stuck on the division of Sindh. During the sixty-seven years partnership of UK and US in Pakistan, especially their engagement in Afghanistan in the proxy war against USSR, both have been favoring Punjabis and strengthened Punjabi dominated Pakistan Army on the cost of ethnic nations Sindhi, Baloch, Pashtun and Siraiki. Sindh is the largest economic contributor of Pakistan. Balochistan and Sindh together form the natural resource richest belt in South Asia. Pakistani establishment that is predominantly Punjabi has developed Punjab and Punjabi dominated military on the resources as well as at the cost of Sindh and Balochistan. Thousands have been killed in both of the provinces in last three decades by the armed forces. A highly massive freedom movement is going on in Sindh, which gathered more than five million Sindhis in Karachi on March 23, 2014 and demanded the international community's intervention for the freedom of Sindh. There is also an armed struggle in Sindh; however it has never attacked a human target. Meanwhile, Baloch are waging a full-scale freedom war in Balochistan since 1999 against the occupation of Punjab. Crimes against humanity, genocides and ethnic cleansing have alarmed the people of conscience around the globe.

Possible role of the UK, being successor of the Great Britain, is historically responsible for the ill-designs and mishaps it has committed while departing from the colonies after the Second World War. It should feel more responsible to the oppressed nations in Pakistan whom British invaded as independent and sovereign countries and later on annexed them with the Pakistan against their will. British should also revise its policies and engagement within Pakistan and think undoing the blunders it has committed during 1947 and later on, whose cost is being paid by the Sindhi, Baloch, Pashtun and Siraiki people in Pakistan.

Published in Daily Afghanistan Times

CO-OPTION OF PAKISTAN: A NEW CHINA PERSPECTIVE

Pakistan has kicked off a new chapter in its strategic as well as economic history, which essentially can be dubbed as *Sinofication* (Chinization) of Pakistan society and state. This would be first-ever initiative over seventy years history of the country that Pakistan has decided a major and futuristic shift in its strategic policy and planning. In 2015, Pakistan and China launched China-Pakistan Economic Corridor (CPEC) worth Chinese investment as well as interest free debt of US$ 46 billion. CPEC consists of several projects of roads, pipelines and energy infrastructure. Both countries have signed 51 agreements and memoranda, which also includes US$ 33 billion investments in energy sector and a US$ 44 million communication strategic project of China-Pakistan fiber optical cable. The project connects China with Gawadar and Karachi Ports through road infrastructure.

The major concern for China is oil security through this mega-engagement in Pakistan. The project would reduce the distance between China and Africa as well as with Europe. This is four-fold plan that includes Gawadar Port, transport infrastructure, energy and industrial cooperation. The Chinese engagement with Pakistan has promising as well as grey areas for the people of Pakistan.

Transformation of Pakistan

Some experts foresee that such a mega investment would transform Pakistan society in terms of political economy. Pakistan faces a decline in foreign investment. It also faces economic instability, particularly due to rising unemployment. It is said that through CPEC 700,000 jobs would be created, which would change the face of Pakistan society. Pakistan already confronts inter-provincial disagreements over distribution of resources, excessive centralization and one province's monopoly over resources, employment and over state structures. This project would potentially create further economic cushion for Punjab province through projects and employment opportunities. This would probably further intensify the conflict among Pakistani federating provinces. Such apprehension has been expressed through statements by the Chief Minister of Sindh. CPEC is no doubt a major economic engagement and creation of job opportunities that could transform Pakistan society; however it seems that the transformation would limit itself to the Punjab province. There arena doubt some aspects of infrastructure development that would have long-term sociologically affects whole Pakistan. It is the political economy of the country that would decide whether these impacts are positive and inclusive for all. Challenges Pakistan is readying 4000 security personnel to protect Chinese personnel in Punjab province who would be involved in different projects under CPEC.

The pool of Chinese security component in Pakistan would rise to 21000, up from 17000 already providing security to the Chinese. Chinese engineer and officials involved in various projects in Balochistan are already facing serious security risks. Pakistani armed forces has undertaken various military operations against secessionists in Balochistan during last couple of decades; the latter have suffered serious setbacks. However, the Baloch secessionists are still strong enough to resist CPEC and there are possibilities that the road construction and other projects may be delayed due to the Baloch insurgency. China also plans to use ports of Sindh. Apart from CPEC, China intends to open about 17000 industrial units in Sindh. This would further cause non-Sindhi migration into towards Sindh from Punjab. Sindhi people are already protesting against Zulfiqarabad project. The government has recently allocated 50 thousand acre land for Bahriya town in Karachi, a project by armed forces to construct settlement facilities for hundreds of thousands.

It is expected that Sindh nationalism would protest against further marginalization of Sindhi people reacting to the possibility of hegemony of one province (Punjab) in the context of CPEC. There are possibilities that Sindhi nationalists may launch people's movements. Meanwhile, the possibilities of disturbance by religious extremists in Khyber Pakhtunkhwa province are almost non-existent. Strategic Isolation Pakistan is feared to further tilt towards China and isolate itself in the regional perspective. Pakistan would have benefited from CPEC if it would have engaged with other international actor's economic interests.

The Afghanistan scenario and the developments in the region suggest that there are possibilities that in the long term, delayed development in Gawadar Port may limit Chinese activities amid communication insecurities. Recently, Iran and India have signed 12 agreements worth US$ 500 million including for the Chahbahar Port project. Besides, a three-way transit accord was signed among Iran India-Afghanistan. It seems that land-locked Afghanistan would strategically inch towards Iran in the context of Chahbahar and Bandar Abbas. This would further isolate Pakistan in the region regarding its designs to choke Afghanistan and Central Asia in the context of their dependency of Gawadar and Karachi Ports. This probably would give fillip to the Taliban insurgency in Afghanistan. Conclusion CPEC is the major strategic and economic shift in Pakistan's seven decades history of statecraft and foreign policy after its alliance with USA against

Soviet Union. Pakistan's internal factors, political economy, federal conflicts, and the absence of progressive economic policy would reduce the benefits of CPEC. Regional developments may isolate Pakistan in the wake of CPEC in the Central and South Asia. There are possibilities that Pakistan would go Chinized in the coming decades. *Published in India Foundation Journal May-June 2016 Issue.*

PAKISTANI OFFICIALS CONFESSED MI PAKISTAN ACTS AS S.L.A.

Since 2013 ISI, RAW and CIA through a modern technology has been talking me as well as with each other apart from fatal attacks and torture on me by certain ISI officials.

In last a few days, Military Intelligence (MI) Pakistan officials in this process has confessed that Sindh / Sindhudesh Liberation (SLA) is nothing but the activities of MI Pakistan to create harassment.

This, they have been doing, to resist recruitment of Sindhi in Pakistan armed forces, ISI, MI and other departments of federal government including intention and practices to induct Punjab(I) Police cadres in the Sindh Police.

Besides, MI Pakistan by doing this has been creating a false justification to present a violent face of Sindh rights movements as well as to victimize different sorts of Sindhi leadership.

Earlier, during this process certain ISI officials ethnically Punjabi however confessed stealing of small nuclear bomb(s), storing of these in seminary (ies) and expressed their intention to nuke Gujarat (India) Sindh, Kabul and USA.

CHINA-PAKISTAN: WHAT LAYS AHEAD FOR SINDH AND REST OF THE WORLD?

Finally, the nightmare has begun. As it was expected, the proposed Chinese intervention in Sindh and Balochistan has greeted the people of Balochistan and Sindh with the Pakistan Air Force bombardment in at least seven districts of Balochistan and two districts of Sindh. It seems that the way Pakistan Army intends to launch the projects would give rise to civil wars and an unending conflict between Pakistan Establishment and the people of Sindh and Balochistan. No doubt, people of Sindh and Balochistan (both are historical countries) would always prioritize their freedom from Pakistan since the people of Sindh and Balochistan have expressed their will for the freedom, and are fighting for it peacefully in Sindh and through freedom war in Balochistan.

No doubt, Sindhi and Baloch are correct while thinking that both can never enjoy their rights, sovereignty, peace and wealth within the framework of Pakistan. However, if this discussion is seen for the moment in the framework of Pakistan, by analyzing some assumed options, things may be having different aspects. Why I am including the other options as well? Because until Pakistan exists, Sindhi and Baloch should never and can never withdraw the governance of their historical motherlands. Therefore, until and unless freedom of Sindh and Balochistan is not practically achieved, federalists in the both would never and should never leave the path for more autonomy, development, security and maximum provincial sovereignty especially through those who believe in the maximum provincial autonomy. And, if something really tangible comes out of it, the Baloch and Sindhi people, who are freedom mongers, would be having space for thinking around it.

Probably, there may be some Western and Asian countries that might have been supporting the people of Sindh and Balochistan silently through diplomatic channels; however, USA is the only country in the world that has been talking for on various occasions for the rights of Sindh. Besides, unfortunately many countries' development funding in Pakistan has not been directed to greater extent for Sindh and Balochistan. Therefore, Sindhi and Baloch have a natural cushion to those who either have been sympathizing Sindhi and Baloch openly like USA and UK (UK has so far been showing its concerns for Balochistan only). Unfortunately, a larger number of the world has remained silent on what has been happening in Sindh and Balochistan; therefore if those who are interested in Sindh and Balochistan needs to give their expression for the rights violation and victimization of Sindhi and Baloch.

No doubt, in any way, Sindhi people are obliged to listen to the countries that have been showing the legitimate concern publicly or diplomatically against the human rights violation and other forms of victimization of Sindh and Balochistan. Since the recent air strikes in Balochistan and Sindh by Pakistani Armed Forces are directly associated with Chinese intervention; therefore the people of Sindh and Balochistan are looking at the world outside to raise pressure on Pakistan for stopping such actions.

China

So far as China is concerned, it has enormous interest in Sindh; however unfortunately China has never taken public and hidden initiatives that could have helped support Sindh and Balochistan for their justified will to sustain and acquire sovereign rights within the Federation of Pakistan. The history hitherto tells that China has been supporting Punjabi military establishment since last seven decades. It is quite clear that this fifteen years long process of implementing Chinese projects would be impossible until people of Sindh and Balochistan agree on it. Therefore, if China is really interested in the projects, it needs to ensure Sindhi and Baloch following guarantees at least:

1. A full-stop to Pakistan Armed Forces Action in Sindh and Balochistan;

2. Separate agreements with the Provincial Governments concerning the projects which may give them guarantees;

3. China also needs to ensure that no initiatives in future would be taken by Punjab that may further tighten the colonization of Sindh, Balochistan and Pakhunkhuwa.

Conclusion

I think, so far the internal dynamics of the issues is concerned; no project can be completed without this; or if completed by the use of force, it will always face the threat of instability. Finally, it seems that like previously China would sideline with the Punjabi military establishment of Pakistan; hence this is almost non-existent option so far. In case China really thinks about changing its policy towards internal affairs of Pakistan, Sindhis should have space for thinking on it. Therefore, Sindhi and Baloch people have to look for the sympathizers, allies and friends from across the world that can be countries, rights bodies and Sindh and Balochistan friendly persons to resist the upcoming permanent of colonization process. Nations use to take decisions on the ground realities, pragmatic, material and practical options, not on the assumptions and reading beyond the mature possibility. Therefore, people and the leadership of Sindh and Balochistan have to see this situation in open, broader and wider matrix. Yes, Sindh needs more friends at this stage, and the tomorrow. We just cannot afford the reduction in the number of our sympathizers and friends. We have to expect hearing from almost all stakeholders. I have a serious question. Why world cannot support the people of Sindh and Balochistan against stopping war crimes by Pakistan in both of the province through diplomatic pressure; or supporting both people on the similar lines of Libya, South Sudan, Kosovo and East Timor?

Published in Merinew, India

ETHNIC CLEANSING: THE EXCEPTIONAL CASE OF PAKISTAN

Destructive forces of history can never act positively. Their fulfillment always finds negative, devastating and perverted means. A review of five thousand years human history indicates that such crimes have always been committed by the uncivilized, brutal and pagan forces in Persian Empire, Roman Empire, Mesopotamia, and during the world wars. Ethnic cleansing In the post second world war globe, some countries have earned (de) fame for war mongering, mass killings and devastation; however those countries have two particular edges - one, they have been doing this in the foreign lands alone and after providing certain true or fallacious justifications; two, they have been doing that by waging an open war.

No other country than that of Pakistan is the only destructive and nihilist force of the post second world war human history, which has the worst ever record of committing larger scale crimes against humanity, committing genocides, homicides, cultural and ethnic cleansings, massacres, apartheid and collective massive gang raps. If someone compiles data of the crimes committed by Pakistan against its citizenry mostly on ethnic and on religious-cum-sectarian lines, as well as against the citizenry of South Asian and some Asian countries, the data would roughly exceed the collective figures of ethnic cleansing committed by Nazis against Jews, Ottoman Turks against Armenian Christians and Colonial Britain against Aboriginals in Australia, Indians of undivided India, and blacks of South Africa. In fact the political history of Pakistan in the context of human rights is the sixty-eight years history of the worst and heinous crimes against humanity in Bangladesh, Sindh, Balochistan, Khyber Pakhtunkhuwa, Siraiki South Punjab, Gilgit-Baltistan, and Pakistan Occupied Kashmir. This also includes the ethnic cleansing and massacres through covert terrorist activities within Pakistan as well as outside in the countries like Afghanistan, India, Thailand, Philippines, and some African and non-Asian nations. Human Cleansing The term 'ethnic cleansing', 'genocide', 'massacre' or 'cultural cleansing' alone does not appropriately represent the criminal history of Pakistan's Muslim-Punjabi military colonialism.

The reason behind finding a new term lies in the multiple massive criminal acts that caused murder of more than a million, rape of hundreds of thousands, enforced disappearances and arbitrary detentions directly by the armed forces; massacres carried out by state-sponsored terrorists and militias; single ethnicity dominated establishment's designs to turn ethnically indigenous nations into minorities in their own historical land through land and residential schemes; employments and inter-provincial migrations; curbs on cultural activities; usurping fiscal, economic, land, water and natural resources; and in some cases organizing crime to de-stablize societies. All this has been done against the various historical nations that unfortunately today are part of Pakistan. Bengali, Baloch, Sindhi, Pashtun, Siraiki and Blaour of Gilgit-Baltistan can never forget sixty-eight years of history of state crimes against humanity in Pakistan. Some main actions of human cleansing: - Creation of Pakistan on August 14, 1947. - Dismissal of KP Provincial Assembly and Government in 1947 and Sindh Government in 1948 - Occupation of Balochistan in 1948 - Separation of Karachi from Sindh to establish federal capital 1948 - Imposition of unitary system, and abolition of the status of provinces through announcing One Unit in 1960s. - Distributing hundreds of thousands acres land of Sindh to the Punjabi military and civil bureaucracy and their relatives in the wake of commissioning Guddu and Kotri barrage - Capturing the financial capital of Sindh after imposing unitary (centralized) system and handing over the resources to Pakistani Punjab - Banning the reading and writing in Sindhi and Bengali language - Transferring the archaeological assets of Sindh to the Lahore Museum - Reducing and ending the time for Sindhi language telecast on the Pakistan Television, and reducing the time of Sindhi broadcast on Radio Pakistan - Annexing some Punjab bordering areas of Sindh with Punjab province - Disallowing publishing of voter lists in Sindhi - Practically disallowed the inclusion of Sindhi and Baloch in the sports like Cricket, Hockey and Boxing - Banning the performance of Haj in Sindh that was earlier carried out in district Badin. Poor Sindhis who could not bear the expenses of performing Haj were undertaking the Haj rituals in district Badin locally on the instructions of Sindhi Sufis until 1980s.

The same practice is resisted in Balochistan where Haj was also being carried by the Baloch Sufis known as Zikris - Usurped the water rights of Sindh, construction of Damns on Indus against the will of Sindhi and Baloch - Destroying Indus Delta area, a ecological regulation site that have significant ecological impacts on not only Sindh but also on almost half of Balochistan, Sindh bordering Siraiki districts of Punjab as well as parts of Indian states of Gujarat and Rajasthan. This caused mass migrations, a great loss of habitat - flaura and fauna and economic repercussions on Sindh - Military backed urban and rural land occupation in Sindh and Balochistan, construction of human settlements, and settlement of non-Sindhis in Sindh to convert Sindhis into permanent minority on their own motherland - Organized settlements of illegal foreigners in Sindh from various countries of Asia particularly South Asia - Resisting urbanization of Sindhis, banning their education and employment in the cities - Giving absolute employment space to the non-Sindhis in the employment opportunities in the private and public sector of Sindh - Organizing massacres in Bengal, Sindh, Balochistan, KP , Siraiki South Punjab and Gilgit-Baltistan across sixty-eight years history of Pakistan through state sponsored religious and urban terrorists and criminals that has taken lives of hundred of thousands - Attempts to create hatred between indigenous Sindhi speaking Sindhi majority and Urdu speaking Sindhi minority - Legislation on ethnically tinted local government laws - Ethnically and religiously tinted administrative decisions - Ethnic cleansing of Sindhi, Balochistani (inclusive of Hazara), Siraiki, Pashtun and Gilgiti Hindus and Shia - Military operations and murders in the torture cells of Pakistan Army of Bengali, Sindhis and Baloch.

These are the major acts of crimes committed by Pakistan during last sixty-eight years that does not only fall in the category of ethnic cleansing and genocide but also have connotations of cultural cleansing, mass raps, collective graves and homicide. Therefore, one can appropriate name it "Human Cleansing". One has to find and adopt a new term for this diversity of mass level mega crimes that also include direct and indirect ethnic cleansing, genocide, massacres and cultural cleansing. Responsibility of the world In this particular situation, it is responsibility of the human conscience, international community, United Nations and rights fraternity of activists in the world to urgently look at this exclusive case of mega scale crimes against humanity, which have no resemblance anywhere in the post second world war global human society.

Published in Merinews, India

SINDH-BALOCHISTAN: PARTICIPATION IN PAKISTAN MILITARY AND SECURITY

Asia's largest military concentration in Sindh

Asia's largest military concentration is in Sindh and Balochistan by Pakistan armed forces and services. If compared with the population vis-a-vis vast terrain in Balochistan, the military-civilian ratio in Balochistan, as well as in Sindh would be alarming. Ethnic composition of armed forces and services: If Pakistani Armed Forces, Army, Navy and Air Forces, Pakistan Rangers, Frontier Constabulary, Coast Guards, and Specially Trained Commandoes in Balochistan are combined with Inter Service Intelligence (ISI) and Military Intelligence (MI), as well as Nuclear and Missile Programs; they form Military Security Regime of Pakistan. Pakistan's Nuclear and Missile Programs are almost non- civilian. Ethnic Punjabi overwhelming majority is there in these forces, services and departments. If expenditures of these are combined, they form largest portion of Pakistan budget. Sindh alone has been bearing these expenditures annually since last seven decades through its natural resources alone excluding Thar coal reservoirs. In fact Uranium and Plutonium from Sindh is being exploited and exported since last four decades by Pakistan authorities. Plutonium is no doubt costliest metal on the earth. Besides, Gold and Copper is being exploited from Iran bordering districts of Balochistan since over two decades. The retired officials of three armed forces, Pakistan Rangers and Frontier Constabularies, ISI, MI, Nuclear, and Missile program take their pensions, perks and benefits from civil / non-defense budget of Pakistan. If this alone is combined, the defense budget of Pakistan overshadows and dominates the thin strip of civilian budget. Sindh is largest contributor of Pakistan economy and resources, followed by Balochistan. If ethnic composition of the Pakistan Army, other armed forces, services and departments is reviewed Sindhi and Baloch are non-existent. Sindhi and Baloch are almost nonexistent in Sindh Regiment and Baloch Regiment of the Pakistan Army. They are nonexistent in EME (Army Engineering / Technical) Corps, Koh Paiman (the mountain defenders); Artillery, Signals Corps, and other formations, divisions and units of Pakistan Army. No ethnic-indigenous Sindhi has been elevated to the post of Brigadier General in Pakistan Army over seven decades, and only one Baloch General, (Lt. General retired Abdul Qadir Baloch) an exception, a few Pashtun Generals from Balochistan, and some Urdu speaking Sindhi and Sindhi of Punjabi origin Generals from Sindh have been there. Only one Air Martial (Air Martial Daudpota) was Sindhi in Pakistan's Air Forces history. General Abdul Qadir Baloch was retired; however he was qualifying the post of Deputy Chief of Army and Air Martial Daudpota was sent to Africa although he was eligible to become Air Chief Marshal. An ethnic-indigenous Sindhi Colonel, (Col. Lakhyar), and exception, was eligible to become Brigadier General in 2006, but an ant was inserted in his record therefore he has not been elevated to the post of Brigadier General until 2012 according to the information of the writer. The Pakistan Army informally claimed with the author that there are roughly one hundred thousand of Sindhis in the Army, which according to author's information are Pakistan is said to have 1 million standing Army, out of that bellow 5 per cent are Sindhi and Baloch each from Sindh and Balochistan provinces.

Asia's largest military concentration: Pano Aqil Cantonment is the largest military installation in Pakistan. And, probably is the largest standing Army in the non-bordering zone at one place in the Asia. It is also the largest military installation at the place, Sindhi, where no military conflict is underway. There are two cantonments in Karachi; one each in Ghtoki in northern Sindh; Hyderabad in Southern Sindh, Petaro in Southern central Sindh; Chhor in Umrekot of Thar desert districts. New as well as up-gradation of / to cantonments are planned in Badin, Tando Allahyar and Sangha districts. Divisions, Brigades, and units are installed in Nawab shah, Dadu, Noshehro, Khairpur Mirs, Larkana, Mithi, Matyari and some other parts of the Sindh. The bordering security force and agency, Pakistan Rangers - Sindh is installed in bordering districts of Badin, Mithi, Umerkot, Sangha, Khairpur Mirs and Ghotki in Sindh. Meanwhile, they are stationed in the various districts as second tier force with certain extent of policing powers in the districts of Karachi East, Karachi West, Karachi, South, District Malir, Hyderabad, Shikarpur, Larkana, Dadu, Naushehro, Jaccobabad, Kashmor, Ghotki, Sangha, Nawabshah, Matyari, Tando Mohammad Khan, TandoAllahyar, Thatta, Badin, Jamshoro, Mithi and Umerkot, almost all districts of Sindh. Largest Naval installations of Pakistan Navy are in Karachi, Sindh and adjoining Lasbella district of Balochistan; however Navy is also there in some other parts of Balochistan. The Pakistan Air Force has installations in Karachi, Sukkur, Jaccobabad as well as some other parts in Sindh; meanwhile Pakistan Coast Guards - Sindh are based in Karachi and Southern towns of Balochistan. The Pakistan Army has cantonments in Quetta, Dera-Bugi-Sibi, Kohluand Khuzdar districts of Balochi speaking Balochistan as well as cantonment for the coastal southern Balochistan, besides Pashtun majority districts of northeastern Balochistan. Pakistan Army's Brigades (formations), Divisions, and Units are in all districts of Balochistan. Construction of some new cantonments is also underway. Frontier Constabulary - Balochistan is installed and stationed in all Afghanistan and Iran bordering districts of Balochistan. Specially trained commando units of Pakistan Army to counter freedom fighters are installed in Quetta, Khuzdar, Qalat and Panjgur. The Pakistan Air Force has also existence in Balochistan. Balochistan's population is below 20 million and Sindh population is between 50 to 60 million according to independent estimates. If military installations in Sindh and Balochistan with reference to the number of Armed forces, and civilian population is compared, it can be validly claimed that Asia's largest military installations are in each Sindh and Balochistan.

Ethnic indigenous Sindhi and Baloch in particular and Sindh born Sindhi of Urdu and Punjabi origin in general, and ethnic indigenous Baloch and to certain extent Pashtuns are thin minority / non-existent in the armed services like Inter-Services-Intelligence (ISI), Military Intelligence (MI) / Federal Investigation Unit (FIU), Pakistan Navy Intelligence, Pakistan Air Force Intelligence, Pakistan Rangers Intelligence, and Frontier Constabulary Balochistan intelligence, and Pakistan Coast Guard's smallest intelligence gathering section. On the similar lines, Sindhi, Baloch and Balochistani Pashtuns are non-existent the strategic departments of defense and communications like Foreign Services / Office, Dr. A.Q. Khan Research Laboratory and other Nuclear Programs as well as Missile Programs including Pakistan Upper Space Research department. Conclusion: The situation has four aspects:

1. Asia's largest military concentration is in each Sindh and Balochistan province in Pakistan.

2. Sindhi, Baloch and Balochistani Pashtun, especially ethnic-indigenous population are non-existent in their share in the defense, security, and civil and non-civil strategic engagements. Sindhi and Balochistani are not allowed to protect their borders, population, land, interests and take participation in strategic developments, and foreign policy.

3. Sindh and Balochistan are largest economic, financial and fiscal contributors for Pakistan, especially in the ethnic-Punjabi dominated center.

4. Sindh is the only province in Pakistan that is using civil-nuclear powerhouse in Karachi, in which Sindhi are not employed. This facility is using Sindh reservoirs of Uranium. This Karachi based facility is in a situation that a Chernobyl like situation can happen at any time, according to a Sindhi newspapers and a Sindh High Court petition.

5. Since Sindh and Balochistan are popularly having secessionist / freedom movements, and since Sindhi-Baloch are not part of Pakistani armed forces and services as well as strategic developments, therefore people of Sindh and Balochistan will not support Pakistan in case of any war is imposed on / waged against Pakistan.

Zulfiqar Shah is a Sindh refugee journalist, analyst and activist currently staying in Delhi, India. He for a shorter period during youth was trained by Commando Unit of Baloch Regiment, Pakistan Army as non-military and civilian student.

Published in Merinews, India

POLITICAL PARTIES IN SINDH

Sindh is history of struggles and peoples movement after partition of undivided India and creation of Pakistan on August 14, 1947. Peoples movements in Sindh have remained around democracy, territorial freedom, provincial autonomy, social and economic justice, culture and language as well as for the other rights and interests of Sindh and Sindhi. Political parties in Sindh today are the dynamic leading aspects of social movements in Sindh. A brief view about Sindh political parties:

Pakistan Peoples Party - Sindh (PPP-Sindh): Largest popular as well as majority parliamentarian political party in Sindh that has never been in minority in Sindh Assembly after 1971.

Founded by martyred Prime Minister Zulfiqar Ali Bhutto and later on led by martyred Prime Minister Benazir Bhutto, PPP has ruled Sindh. Current Sindh Government is led by PPP. PPP has a history of leading Movement for Restoration of Democracy (MRD) in 1981 - 1988 in Sindh against military regime of General Ziaul Haq and Sindh rights. Hundreds of PPP activists were jailed and trialed in the military courts during the movement. Some were killed. Syed Ali Murad Shah, Chief Minister of Sindh; Qaim Ali Shah, Nisar Khuhro; Sassui Palejo and others lead the party in Sindh.

Jeay Sindh Qomi Mahaz (Bashir Qureshi)– JSQM: Second largest popular and street power political party of Sindh that does not take part in the parliament elections. JSQM is one of the successors early of 1970s political movement that was for the territorial freedom of Sindh. JSQM held three Sindh Freedom Marches in Karachi participated by hundreds of thousands of Sindhi for the liberation of Sindh. JSQM leader Bashir Qureshi was poisoned to death and another leader Maqsood Qureshi was killed by the secret agencies / forces. A considerable number of JSQM activists have been killed over last two decades; hundreds have been enforcedly disappeared, as well as illegally arrested as well as jailed during its history.

JSQM today is led by Sunan Qurshi and others.

Mujtahid Qomi Movement (MQM): MQM is the third largest political party in Sindh from the popular as well as parliament representation perspective. The largest number of MQM membership is among Urdu speaking Sindhi whose ancestors refuged in Sindh from India after creation of Pakistan. They claim themselves Muhajirs (refugees / immigrants). MQM previously has been focusing on urban - rural divide and had illegitimately demanded division of Sindh. Their stronghold is in Urdu speaking minority of Karachi. MQM activists have also been enforced disappeared, killed, arrested and jailed over last two decades. MQM has also been said to be involved in violence in Karachi. MQM is led by Altaf Hussain, living in exile in UK and by Farooq Sattar living in Karachi, Sindh.

Pakistan Muslim League Functional (PML – F): PML-F is fourth largest political party of Sindh lad by spiritual leaders of those who took part in the World War II and fought two wars for the freedom of Sindh during 1890-1899 and 1942-1943. PML-F has dwindled between second and third largest political party in Sindh Assembly. PML-F majority membership is Hur Sindhi community. It is led by Pir Pagaro and his brother Syed Saddaruddin Shah Rashidi.

Qomi Awami Tahreek (QAT): QAT has a four decades legacy of struggles for the provincial autonomy, democracy and Sindh rights. A left leaning party, QAT has been considered the core leading and organizing political party of the Movement for the Restoration of Democracy (MRD) in Sindh. QAT, a continuation of Awami Tahreek and Awani National Party (ANP)'s Sindhi membership, has apart from others, leading contribution in movement against construction of Kalabagh Dam and for Sindh Water Rights. Some QAT activists have been killed hitherto, hundreds enforced disappeared, illegally arrested and jailed. QAT is continuation of the movement lead by legendry Rassol Bux Palejo and is led by his son Ayaz Lateef Palejo and others.

Sindh Taraqi Passand Party (STP): STP has three decades history of struggle for provincial autonomy and Sindh rights. Some of STP activists have been killed, hundreds arrested and many jailed during its history. STP previously was vociferous against settlement of non-Sindhi in Sindh. STP is founded and led by Dr. Qadir Magsi, and is led others that includes Dr. Rajib Memon, a scholar.

Sindh United Party (SUP): SUP has two decades history for the struggle for the sovereign autonomy of Sindh. Many of its activists have been illegally arrested and jailed. SUP is led by Syed Jalal Mehmood Shah, grandson of legendry G. M. Syyed.

Jeay Sindh Qomi Mahaz - (Arisar JSQM-A) JSQM-A is one of the successors of early 1970s political movement that was for the territorial freedom of Sindh. JSQM-A has been struggling for the freedom of Sindh and has been protesting on various issues. A considerable number of JSQM activists have been killed over last two decades; hundreds have been enforcedly disappeared and illegally arrested during its history. JSQM-A today is led by Mir Alam Mari and others. Its founding leader was renown leader and scholar late Abdul Wahid Arisar.

Pakistan Muslim - League Nawaz Sharif (PML-N Sindh): PML-N Sindh is mostly focused on parliamentary politics in Sindh where it has been wining on limited seats; however once it got considerable seats and formed Sindh government. PML-N has history of participation in the restoration movement for the Chief Justice of Pakistan Iftekhar Ahmed Chaudhry and release of Nawaz Sharif. A large number of Punjabi that are settled in Sindh vote PML-N. It is led by Ghaus Ali Shah (Sindhi), Haleem Adil Siddiqui (Punjabi), Ghulam Murtaza Jatoi (Sindhi) and others.

Jeay Sindh Mujtahid Mahaz (JSMM): JSMM is one of the successors of early 1970s political movement that was for the territorial freedom of Sindh. JSMM has been struggling for the freedom of Sindh and has been protesting on various issues. Many JSMM activists have been killed over last two decades; hundreds have been enforcedly disappeared and illegally arrested as well as jailed during its history. JSMM today is led by Shafi Burfat who according to newspapers is in exile.

Jeay Sindh Tahreek (JST): JST is one of the successors of early 1970s political movement that was for the territorial freedom of Sindh. JST has been struggling for the freedom of Sindh and has been protesting on various issues. Some of the JST activists have been killed over last one decade; a large number have been enforcedly disappeared, illegally arrested as well as jailed during its history. JST is led Dr. Safdar Sarki, Fatah Channa and others. A splinter group of JST was also led by Shafi Karnani who was killed in 2016 by state sponsored murderers.

Pakistan Peoples Party Shaheed Bhutto - Sindh (PPP SB Sindh) PPP SB is splinter group of Pakistan Peoples Party founded by Murtaza Bhutto, a popular leader and parliamentarian. He was son of martyr Prime Minister Zulfiqar Ali Bhutto and brother of martyr Prime Minister Benazir Bhutto. PPP SB shares legacy of struggles by Pakistan Peoples Party until mid-1990s. It is led by Ghinwa Bhutto, a Bruit born wife of Murtaza Bhutto. Zulfiqar Bhutto Junior is next in the queue of leadership.

Jeay Sindh Mahaz - Riaz Chandio (JSM): JSM is one of the successors of early 1970s political movement that was for the territorial freedom of Sindh. JSM has been struggling for the freedom of Sindh and has been protesting on various issues. Many JSM activists have been enforcedly disappeared, as well as illegally arrested during last one decade. JSM is led by Riaz Chandio.

Jeay Sindh Mahaz - Abdul Khaliq Junejo (JSM): JSM is one of the successors of early 1970s political movement that was for the territorial freedom of Sindh. JSM has been struggling for the freedom of Sindh and has been protesting on various issues. Many JSM activists have been enforcedly disappeared, illegally arrested and jailed during last three decade. JSM is led by Abdul Khaliq Junejo, Hashim Khoso and others.

Muhajir Qomi Movement Haqqiqi (MQM-H): MQM H is a political party that is in some residential areas of Karachi and Hyderabad cities of Sindh. MQM H is led by Afaq Ahmed. MQM-H also known as MQM Afaq / MQM -A was formed when Muhajir Qomi Movement (MQM) was splinted into two – Mujtahid Qomi Movement and Muhajir Qomi Movement. Many MQM – H activists have been killed, arrested and jailed in last two decades. It has been demanding for the division of Sindh.

Sindh National Movement (SNM): SNM was founded by renown activist and leader late Ali Hassan Chandio. SNM has its existence in some Sindhi speaking parts of Karachi and Hyderabad as well as rest of the Sindh. SNM has been struggling since last some years for the provincial autonomy and issues of Sindh.

Sindhi Adabi Sangat (SAT): Sindhi Adabi Sangat is largest Sindhi literati forum that has focus on Sindhi language and literature. It has at least three decades history of the struggle for Sindhi language.

There are also some other political parties and groups in Sindh that include Communist Party of Pakistan, Sindh; Workers Party; Sindh Sagar Party and Jeay Sindh Inqlabi Party.

Jamiat-e-Ulmeai Islam - Fazul Rehman Sindh (JUI-F Sindh): JUI-F Sindh is right wing religious political party, mostly having its pocket in some areas of the northern Sindh. It also has members in the Parliament. JUI-F has history of struggle against Kalabagh Dam, and for natural resources rights of Sindh. Murder of JUIF leader Dr. Khalid Mehmood Sommro was due to JUI-F Sindh plans of struggle for the natural resources rights of Sindh.

Awami National Party Sindh (ANP Sindh): ANP-Sindh has two streams of history. Earlier, until 1988 it was one of the popular political parties in Sindh. ANP-Sindh today is limited to the Pashtun immigrants from Khyber Pakhtunkhuwa (KP) province to Sindh. It mainly is in Karachi with some branches in Hyderabad and Sukkur. ANP-Sindh has a very recent history of very few (bellow five) members in Sindh Assembly. ANP-Sindh is led by Shahi Syed.

Jamait-e-Islami Sindh (JI-Sindh): Jam'at Islami Sindhi (JI-Sindh) is a right wing religious political party based on Salafism. JI Sindh is different from rest of JI in Pakistan. JI Sindh has a history of highly limited Parliamentarians from Sindh. Jam'at Islami in Karachi at least once formed local government. Urdu speaking Sindhi (MQM claims this linguistic group Muhajar) forms largest membership of the party. Maulana Asadullah Bhutto is Sindh leader of JI.

Tahreek-e-Inasaf Sindh (TI-Sindh): Tahreek-e-Inasaf Sindh (TI-Sindh) is a recently founded political party that has won seats for Sindh Assembly and National Assembly from Karachi at least. Tahreek-e-Insaf has newly developed itself in the various districts of Sindh. Mr. Alavi and Lal Malhi are among some of its leaders. Sunni Tahreek - Sindh (ST-Sindh) Sunni Tahreek is one of the popular right wing religious parties in Sindh. It has its roots in the urban hubs of Sindh like Karachi, Hyderabad, Sukkur, Mirpur has, and Nawabshah. Urdu speaking Sindhi (MQM claims this linguistic group Muhajor) are the members of this party. Leadership of the party were assassinated more than once.

Communist Party of Pakistan - Sindh (CPP-Sindh): Communist Party of Pakistan has mainly two split groups in Sindh that have their rag tag existence in Urban hubs and trade union of Sindh. In past, it was one of the vibrant left parties in the province. Awami Workers Party - Sindh (AWP-Sindh) AWP - Sindh is a left political party that is a result of merger of several left political parties from across Pakistan including Labour Party Pakistan, Awami Party Pakistan and National Workers Party. It has existence in some urban and rural areas of Sindh.

Pak Saracen Party (Pak Saracen:) Paki Saracen Party is a splinted group from Mujtahid Qomi Movement (MQM) and exists in Karachi, Hyderabad and some other urban parts of Sindh. Led by previous Mayor (Nazim) of Karachi, Mustafa Kamal, Pak Saracen Party was realized after cadres had differences with the rest in MQM. Urdu speaking Sindhi (MQM claims this linguistic group Muhajor) are the members of this party.

Sindh Sagar Party -- Sindh Sagar Party is a political group in some districts of Sindh. It is highly skewed. The party follows Shaikh Obaidullah Sindhi's school of thought. It profess liberal and secular version of Islam and strive for the sovereignty of Sindh.

Pakhtunkhuwa Mili Awami Party - Sindh (PkMP – Sindh): PkMP has highly skewed units and limited memberships within some of Pashtuns that have migrated to Karachi from Balochistan and southeastern Afghanistan.

Published in Merinews, India

CHINA-PAKISTAN AXIS: BEGINNING OF A NEW COLD WAR

China and Pakistan recently have signed over one hundred agreements worth 64 billion USD in the field of infrastructure developments. These projects are mainly connected with the development and operations of the new and old seaports in Sindh and Balochistan as well as initiatives that connect China with coastal strip of these provinces, and also with Afghanistan bordering Khyber Pakhtunkhuwa (KP), India bordering Pakistan invaded Kashmir (PaK) and landlocked Pakistani Punjab. There are some geo-strategic and economic interest perspectives of these projects:

1. China want an easy and uninterrupted outreach near Africa, Europe, Middle East and Iran through Arabian Sea and Afghanistan through low altitude tracks of KP in Pakistan.

2. China also want to give a permanent strategic checkmate to India at its western borders, although it has attempted similar on India's eastern and to certain extent deep southern borders.

3. China will have an edge over the USA, the UK, Russian, India and France interests on the axis of Middle East - Central Asia.

4. China would also remain a permanent check over India's economic and deep future's military coordination with Afghanistan and Iran through Port Abass in Iran.

5. Russia would be left with no other option than to depend on China alone concerning its Central and South Asian interests.

6. Pakistan would regain its bygone strategic and economic importance after assuming these projects.

7. Pakistan is seeing these projects as the last life-line for the existence of country since three and half of the federating province out of four (Sindh, Balochistan, Khyber Pakhtunkhuwa, and ethnic Siraiki southern half of Punjab) and at least people of the two administered units Gilgit-Baltistan and Afghan bordering FATA have expressed their will to secede from Pakistan out of four administrative units (the remaining administrative units are Islamabad's Capital Territory and Pakistan invaded Kashmir).

8. Strategically high important and economic back bone provinces of Pakistan, Sindh and Balochistan, see these projects against the sovereignty as these would not permanently skew options for the freedom for these provinces from the monopoly of ethnic Punjabi Muslims, but also convert the indigenous majority of ethnic Sindhi and Baloch into permanent minorities in there historical motherlands.

Pakistani establishment has also announced gigantic housing schemes in Sindh through the projects of Zulfiqarabad, Bahriya (Navy) Town, Malir Housing projects and others that are meant to transfer 20 million ethnic Punjabis to Sindh and at least 10 million to Balochistan through Guwadar Port. These new developments are potential not only to extremely change the Asiatic and global balance of power, but also is potential to turn the world into bi-polar power matrix and thus giving birth to a new cold war. These developments would also challenge the interests and strategic niche of the European Union, USA, Canada, India, Australia, Japan, Israel, some middle eastern nations, Iran and India. What can be the possible way-outs to address these developments?

1. The possible affected nations outside and inside Pakistan join together against these developments, and people of Sindh and Balochistan are strengthened in their movements for the right to self determination and freedom.

2. USA, Russia and European Unions need an immediate coordination to minimize rifts caused by the Crimean situation.

3. A consensus between and among USA, UK, China, Russia, France, Germany and India over these projects in a bid that the interests of almost all parties stand unchallenged as well as the interests of Sindh and Balochistan are also well addressed.

These new developments are completely unavoidable by and for the world powers and the concerned groups. Simultaneously, the concerns and sovereignty interests of Sindh and Balochistan can also not be avoided. Therefore, a new thinking and a set of new initiatives at large are required.

Published in Merinews, India in 2015

WORLD – A SINDHIST VIEW

CHINA'S ONE ROAD, ONE BELT DEBACLE

China's ambitious One Road, One Belt (OBOR) plan, a road, maritime and railways infrastructure network that would encompass sixty countries and will require the infrastructure investment of US$ 4 to 8 trillion probably prove to be an infrastructure development debacle.

Historically Silk Route belongs to Sindh, which for centuries China, Afghanistan, today's India, Central Asia and Russia were using for the trade. It can be called One Belt One Road of Kingdom of Sindh in yesteryears; however, when slain ex-Prime Minister of Pakistan Benazir Bhutto, a Sindhi, wanted this route to revive and named the scheme Keti Bandar Project, the around sixteen Punjabi speaking districts based security establishment of Pakistan forced rejected it. Later on, all of sudden China's Xi Jiping came with the same idea and earned status of Mao Zedong due to this by the Communist Party of China.

There are some gray areas in plan. OBOR's India, Bangladesh and Myanmar phase is impossible since India is not joining OBOR. Besides, China Pakistan Economic Corridor (CPEC) will not have connectivity with Afghanistan and Central Asia if seen in the context of Pakistan-Afghanistan relations. Pakistan support to Taliban has created conflict between Pakistan and Afghanistan due to which Afghanistan has signed trilateral agreement with Iran and India for connectivity with Chabahar Port in Iran. Afghanistan will prefer to use Chabahar Port in comparison with Guwadar Port, Pakistan. Therefore CPEC the important most project of OBOR will remain restricted to China and its access to Europe and some parts of Africa. OBOR's Nepal phase is bilateral and would connect only China and Nepal. Since India is not participating OBOR, the Nepal part of OBOR would not create land route connectivity with other South Asian countries. Meanwhile, after completing of US$ 57 billion CPEC project, China will reduce its maritime distance with the some African and European countries. The volume of business between China and some African and European countries necessarily has to be at limited scale. After CPEC, recently developed UK-China train service will loose its trade importance because China will have cheaper and nearer connectivity with the Europe through maritime.

Maintenance of this trillion dollar initiatives would be another concern because OBOR will need to generate higher trade volume to meet maintenance cost. Besides, security on the modern times silk route would be another permanent security and financial constrain of the OBOR.

Recently Pakistan ports and shipping minister Mir Hasil Bizanjo told the parliament, "as per the concession agreement, China Overseas Port Holding Company (COPHC) has 91 percent share of revenue collection from the gross revenue of the terminal and marine operations and 85percent share from gross revenue of free zone operation. The provinces have no share in revenue collection as per the constitution." It means along with a peoples movement against CPEC it in Sindh, Balochistan and Khyber Pakhutunkhuwa provinces, province-center conflict will also increase in Pakistan. Recently, an ethnic Pashtun Jirga (tribal representative council) has said that the CPEC is only in the interest of Punjab province and termed CPEC an ethnic "Punjabi Corridor" in Pakistan. Insurgency in Balochistan is underway against the construction of Guwader Port in Balochistan province of Pakistan, and massive peoples' protests are being held in Sindh province against construction of Zulfiqarabad Port. Guwadar and Zulfiqarabad are the key construction sites of CPEC in Pakistan.

China has already purchased 40 percent shares of Pakistan Stock Exchange in December last year and recently Chinese businessmen have set up textile units in Karachi, Sindh in Pakistan, which will create Chinese monopoly on Pakistan economy. Besides, who will invest in China monopolized Pakistan Stock Exchange? Pakistan, against expectations, will not have much touted economic benefits of CPEC.

GLOBAL SECURITY AMID RUSSIA-USA RELATIONS

World faces challenges of stability -- a world in which a better patchwork of alliance may work as a new power matrix to brushstroke Iraq and Afghanistan stability, resolution of Syrian crises, and ensure new geo-economics corridors for collective benefits.

Endgame Afghanistan and Iraq

After annexation of Crimea with Russia, the shift in the global politics worst affected Afghanistan transition; global fight against rouge Islamist elements like Al-Qaida, ISIS and Taliban in Asia and in the rest of the world; and most importantly the situation has put an end to the chapter of USA-Russia consensus over certain issues. World has suffered in Asia, Europe and America at the hands of Taliban, ISIS and Al-Qaida in last three years. The continuous violence in Afghanistan by Taliban and emergence of Islamic State (ISIS) as a terror front has posed question whether twenty-first century world would be able to get rid of this kind of terror directed politics?

Afghanistan is landlocked. Afghanistan, Central Asian Counties and Russia require easy outreach to Indian Ocean and Arabian Sea. Historically, there have been two routs: Ports of Sindh and Balochistan in Pakistan; and Ports Abass in Iran. Without a route towards Indian Ocean and endgame of Taliban and ISIS in Afghanistan, the world peace and geo-economic developments are impossible. Port Abass and Chabahar in Iran are only the way-forwards for Afghanistan, Eurasia and the world with reference to Afghanistan. Gawadar Port will take time for such aspects. In that particular context, USA will be having a new approach towards Iran. An engagement with Iran and a possible engagement regarding management of Iran-Israel issues would be the only solution in that context.

Beyond Traditional Arab Politics

Iran historically has remained distant from typical Arab politics by the Arab countries and violence by the Arab oriented outfits like Al-Qaida and ISIS. Iraq, today, also faces threat of religious violence and does not sideline tradition Arab politics. Turkey historically has remained distant from tradition Arab politics. Timothy of Iraq-Turkey-Iran for the matters related to West Asia would always be a long term solution. It is important to note that Salafi sect of Islam, a tiny minority, hitherto has been threat to world peace mainly in the form of Al-Qaida, ISIS and others. Political Salafism has been in the foundation of Taliban. Shia Muslim, a sect larger than Salafi, has never been a global security challenge, nor has it caused terrorism in the West. Therefore, USA and Russia not only have to work out modus operandi for mutual interests and actions; they have to choose out of Iran and Pakistan an ally in the context of Afghanistan.

China in the world politics

China is great challenge to the Western countries and their allies. Global economy; military security aspects of South China Sea; and Chinese advancement towards African and Asian markets has made a greater security risk to the North America, UK, European Union and Australia. China through China Pakistan Economic Corridor (CPEC) has got and will further get outreach to Indian Ocean and Arabian Sea. China considers India, Japan and South Korea a security threat.

Russia, although a military might, has no particular economic benefit from China. Russia is rather supporting Chinese security and economic niche through Russian role in the world politics and giving geo-economic cushion to the China. These realities further indicate that Russia-USA normalization of relations and alliance on certain issues like ISIS, Al-Qaida and Muslim terrorism between both of the countries would be in the better interests of the world.

Russia-USA ties

A Russia-USA understanding-cum-consensus on certain aspects of global security would result in stability. It will help stabilize Afghanistan and Iraq; finally solve Syrian crises; give an end to Salafi terrorism in the name of Islam; and create better relations for the future economic pathways. Russia must also consider its economic and geo-economic niche as well. Simultaneously, it is a bigger challenge for USA to formulate global policy in which decade long tactical and strategic failure may be turned into success.

WORLD POLITICS, GLOBALIZATION, AND COLLECTIVE HUMAN RESPONSIBILITY

The world faces diverse socio-political, economic and spiritual issues and problems. If this phenomenon of contemporary global disorder is interpreted philosophically, it is a conflict of 'structuralism' versus 'essentialism' within the state, society, and beyond.

The individuality of the issues needs to be analyzed in depth; however without seeing the collective and essential perspective we will find the appropriate and sustainable solutions of the issues.

Structuralism, society and the state

The state, as a social organism, was meant to manage the diversity of affairs of social, national or the entities. The institution of state traces back its embryos to the human family unit of the Neolithic era in the human history. Thus, state is a structural entity with 'essentiality' of the diverse responsibilities. Like many other forms of social organization, it was born out of society but has since been trying to control and regulate the society from which it came.

Generally, discourse on the state-society relations is discouraged and faces curbs as free expression in developing and under developed societies. The only dominant discourse in the state-society relations runs around the military – civil relations particularly because regional and multilateral military engagements have surged in the last two decades around the world.

The same is the problem can be seen around religious practices. Practices of the faithful associated with almost all religions in the world have distanced themselves from the essence of their religions, but have stuck to the structures and traditions built around the religions instead, despite the fact that no sacred book in majority of the religions has described particular order of the structure. In fact, the institutions of Mullahism, Panditism, Priesthood or Monkism are later developments and are not part of the Holy Texts.

The political parties and social movements of our times are also victim of this phenomenon of 'structuralism' and therefore have always proved to be less productive, and eventually create socially and humanly less conducive polity.

If analysed precisely, the issues like increase in militarization, violence, religious extremism, terrorism, wars, intolerance, nepotism, corruption and socio-economic injustice are result of focusing more on structural aspects of the states, governance, religions and social organisms like political parties and social movements.

Globalization: Cold War and today

It is difficult to observe globalised societies before Cold War, as more recent state institutions have dominated the process of globalization. In today's process of globalization, states are more globalised than the common world citizenry as well as social and political movements. Globalization and the enlargement of state institutions through submergence of the broader civil society have also had some positive aspects, such as the relatively greater number of pro-society elements, which are heard in decision-making processes; however on the other hand state gets more leeway to dominate the voices of dissent. Similarly to how the judiciary plays a role in state-society conflicts, broader civil-society provides a neutral cushion in the state-society conflict. However, civil-society is more responsible to the people, while the judiciary is more responsible to the constitution and in many cases the state.

Marxism discussed politics based on themes across international borders, globalizing politics and social movements during the Cold War. And, today's communication and technological revolutions have crossed the borders of national-states and pushed globalization further.

However, terrorism, religious extremism and expansion in the security and intelligence services around the world have reduced the physical globalization of human beings. This situation has not only given birth to the visa regime tightness and reduced the area of civil liberties, but also has reduced the broader physical exposure between and among the societies and cultures.

Besides, the war-making process has become more globalised than the peace-making initiatives.

Gradually but steadily health and education sectors; media and foreign policy sectors of societies and states are becoming globalised; however shared human wisdom and developments as well as sharing between cultures and civilizations are the requirement of our times. Without these, a new global order would be impossible.

Mutually assured destruction

The two-decades long reality of world politics have remained the real concern of the global citizenry. No doubt, some of the wars were unavoidable during last three decades despite their basis on previous foreign policy mistakes, but some were avoidable and unnecessary. For example, had the war on terrorism been focused on Pakistan instead of Afghanistan and Iraq in the wake of 9/11, it may have provided more sustainable results.

When world players choose actions that are more exhaustive and less result oriented, they create a situation like that of Mutually assured destruction (MAD). The idea of MAD is visible in international terror organizations, and it is important most for the forces against terrorism that they avoid becoming victims of the same ideas, as those ideas are what brought two world wars in the first half of the last century.

Collective human responsibility

Some of the nations around the world remained subjugated after Second World War. The instruments of their subjugation can be split into three categories: agreements; invasions; and the decisions of ex-colonizers. The world today is collectively responsible to these subjugated nations, and a framework needs to be developed to address these three different categories.

Some of the nations won freedom during cold war, rest at the end cold war and a few in and around the first decade of the twentieth century. The legitimate case of remaining a few like Kurdistan in Iraq, and Sindh and Balochistan in Pakistan (avoiding to mention Tibet because Dalai Lama has been focussing on the Provincial Autonomy since last decade) at least needs to considered by the international community.

What else?

Better initiatives by some of the regional powers might have left highly positive impacts on the regional and the world politics. Had Kingdom of Saudi Arabia (KSA), for instance, chosen to form Saudi Peacekeeping Forces under United Nations especially for the conflict resolution either across the world or in the *Salafism* majority / friendly countries or societies (or the conflict in which KSA have not been party) it would have not only earned a better reputation but also recognition for it use of soft power.

At the same time, the Organization of Islamic Countries (OIC), which includes many wealthy Muslim countries as members, has only proved to be a forum of meetings. It could have developed a funding mechanism for the countries where Muslim communities live in a bid to eradicate poverty, illiteracy and health issues, as well as addressing natural and man-made calamities.

Meanwhile, in today's highly sensitive and volatile environment around the religions, none have thought to reach an agreement, which turns sacred places into war and violence free zones. These can include but not limited to Church of Nativity and Bethlehem (Israel), Vatican City (Rome), Mecca and Medina (Kingdom of Saudi Arabia), Varanasi (India), the birthplace of Buddha (Nepal), centres of Taoism and Confucianism (China), and shrines of Imams (Iran, Iraq and Syria) as well as UNESCO recognized world heritage sites as well and UN recognized Ramsar Sites. At the same time, United Nations that has given space to the individuals or the group of the individuals for petitioning against state parties concerning some issues, has created no room for the nations, territorial entities and ethnic groups that aspire freedom or secession.

This kind of issue becomes highly important when it become an established reality that majority of the certain ethnic nation that have remained a historically sovereign country wants freedom. It also requires especial focus in the countries that either do not give such rights to federating provinces, state or territories or have remained under military rules. There needs to be forum in the United Nations in which the ruling or opposition political parties of such nations or territories or the broader civil society in the wake of ethnic crimes as well as extreme civil, political and economic rights violation may petition for UN intervention concerning the secession / liberation.

Conclusion

Most of the issues in our times are caused by the dominance of the structure over the essence in and between state and society, and within the various social organizations like religious outfits, political parties and social movements. Not only is a new discourse required around 'structuralism versus essence' in the world politics, but a concrete way forward is also needed for the more positive, productive and result oriented world politics.

Published on Descrier, UK

FOREIGN POLICY OF OPPRESSED

Foreign policy is not only a matter of the nations that are having a sovereign country. There use to be a foreign policy of oppressed as well, which usually is carried out by the social and public faces as well as intelligentsia of the social movements, oppressed nations or the nations without states. There is one fundamental principle in the foundations of the foreign policy of oppressed: The social, political, cultural and intellectual leadership and representation of that nation / social movement must be knowing the broader outlines of the interests of the nation and the basics of international as well as peoples diplomacy or the borderless diplomacy. Let us discuss this highly academic nature of issue in the form of basic questions because this write-up is the first of its kind on such a theme.

Or let us say, the theme itself has not been discussed academically so far, therefore primarily it requires basic understanding of the things. Who can be considered oppressed people? There are so many social groups and entities that can be considered in the category of oppressed: I. Oppressed and occupied nations that are struggling for freedom, secession, independence, liberation, right to self determination and / or a wider range of rights; II. Discriminated and vulnerable classes and sections of the society like wage-laborers, agriculture workers, fishing communities, hilly and nomadic people; indigenous communities; and significant ethno-linguistic and religious minorities; III. Peculiar sections of the society like gays, lesbians, and trans-gender community. Why oppressed needs a foreign policy? The foreign policy for discriminated and vulnerable as well as peculiar sections and classes of society need an entirely non-confronted foreign policy and engagement to achieve some things in the context of rights regime, legislation and implementation.

Since the social movements of such social sections and classes are usually not considered against the state or the particular construct of the state, but require certain reforms by the state in a bid to attain their fundamental rights both in the society and state; therefore their foreign policies and engagements are very smooth, highly welcomed, simple, issue based and are accommodated mostly by the various groups of power across the world. There is another peculiarity of these groups foreign policy that they have broader options for making friends, form networks and seek support from other similar social movements, groups and institutes. Foreign policy for oppressed as well as stateless nations, and the occupied people is one of the highly patchy, hard, and well resisted initiative. Such foreign policy is usually unwritten, becomes an outcome of collective socio-political and economic understanding of the nations that gradually develops during the course of oppression. This foreign policy engagement is highly resisted by the establishment of the oppressor state and its allied states. It always works around political, economic, social and cultural rights, importance, and interests.

These foreign policy initiatives can be carried on people-to-people, rights bodies, political movements and sympathetic government level. Mostly these initiatives are carried to seek maximum external support, positive perception and lobbying to build pressure on the oppressor state in a hope to seek rights and resolve issues. Who does carry the foreign policy from among the oppressed? Leaders and cadres of political parties as well as movements; civil and political rights activists; writers; journalists; intellectuals; actors; singers and sports persons from among the oppressed usually undertake the foreign policy of the oppressed. However, each groups' engagement has its own nature of initiatives. What are the categories of oppressed people's foreign policies? When political actors undertake foreign policy engagement, they mostly discuss the political, strategic, state, movement and diplomatic support for their cause. They usually engage with the governments, political parties and political movements of the various friendly countries. The engagement by the civil and political rights activists mostly deal the very same issues for which political parties struggle; and are justified under given broader rights instruments and frameworks adopted either by international community and rights groups worldwide or by law of the country in which their nation is being oppressed. However, their method of engagement is highly different from the method of political parties. Writers, journalists and intellectuals of the nations, unlike others, may not adopt travelling requirements like others; however they usually write and discourse on the issues and rights of political movements through writing or spoken as well as visual discourse. They mostly do not associate with any political group. They usually think and express about the broader interests of the people. The cultural representatives of oppressed usually focus on the cultural aspects of the oppressed nation which usually have political relevance in their era's regional, continental and international issues.

Issues versus stance in the oppressed policy?

A foreign policy of oppressed may be divided into two sections. An engagement that is around certain political issues like natural resources exploitation; ethnic cleansing; rights violation; and the engagement that is around sovereign aspects like provincial autonomy; right to self-determination and territorial freedom. Juxtapositions in the foreign policy of oppressed A oppressed nation usually fights on two fronts -- its participation in the governance through votes; and at the same time its struggle for the sovereign and independent status. Some odd times come in the foreign policy of oppressed when secessionist tend to support those who want to seek the rights within federation / oppressor state; and vice versa. And, in some of the perspective both join their hands together. About the subject Since there is no available academic discourse and treatise on the issue, therefore its more details either can come from those who have been part of this process or can be researched furthermore. A detailed research work is required on this subject. To the oppressed There is not only excessive need to get engage in the foreign policy for the oppressed but there is much need to learn from the associates from across the successful movements like East Timor, Kosovo and South Sudan. *Published in Merinews, India*

THE NEW NEUTRAL

When individual or collective conflicts push politics into a blind alley, neutrality becomes key to mediation and resolution. Mediation, in all its forms—cultural, individual, collective or judicial—requires neutrality. If seen through the lens of diplomatic history among nations and the cultural history of people, neutrality embodied with justice has not only been successful in bringing about peace but also sustaining it. Hence, the diversified nature of conflicts, inter- as well as intrastate, ethnic and group require the exhibition of extreme neutrality for a judicious and sustainable resolution of the antagonism that is destined to lead all of us towards collective destruction.

No sides to take
Inter- and intra-state, ethnic and national conflicts have frequently occurred in the post-modern world. The post-World War League of Nations, which culminated into the UN, was an outcome of many international/European treaties among nations, which were neither judicious nor brokered by neutral mediators. Hence, it provided a reason for World War II. The two World Wars were waged between colonizers and aspirants holding colonial ambitions, seeking maximum control over colonies and their wealth and natural resources. Thus, the birth of the UN became inevitable since a neutral body was the niche of the modern era of statehood. Meanwhile, the powerful among the countries also formed parallel alliances at regional and international levels to further their interests.

No doubt, the UN has gradually transcended into a comparatively neutral forum since the world needed to go a step forward to formulate an international legal framework, not only for the member states but also for the citizens of member states. However, it is our duty to introduce further reforms, agree upon new legal and policy frameworks, reform the structure and the authority to exhibit maximum neutrality and impartiality.

Nations, governments and international institutions always have to deal with a complex patchwork of relations and behaviors when they have to switch between neutrality and securing their interests. Since national interest has mostly superseded justice and neutrality in interest-based competitions, diplomacy and internal-external engagements, neutrality today has become an absurdity. This was evident in the recent political crises in Syria and Ukraine. It has also been observed in the Israel-Palestine conflict, the Kurdistan Movement, the Tibetan issue and the freedom movement in Sindh and Balochistan in Pakistan.

In fact, the absence of justice-based neutrality, both in nation-states and international and regional forums like the UN, Saarc and the Organization of Islamic Countries, despite coming up with remedies have also been deepening the old wounds of the people. This has resulted in the rise of gross human rights violations, ethnic cleansing and war crimes that victimize millions of innocent citizens and dissenters.

Power biases
Power and interest-based politics and diplomacy have also given birth to another kind of discrimination. It is based on a discriminatory approach towards social leadership from the perspective of the oppressed or less powerful nations and ethnicities vis-à-vis monopolists and the powerful. The phenomenon is exclusively seen in broader civil society, which includes activists, journalists, writers, analysts, intellectuals, lawyers and other professionals. Usually, social leadership, associated with powerful ethnic groups, command more centrality and acceptability than leaders from among the group of oppressed people.

The phenomenon is more visible in the developing world, particularly in South Asian societies where social, institutional and structural development has historically been built around power. Pakistan, Bangladesh and Nepal are the best examples of this tilt. Since the Pakistani state and power corridors, for example, are monopolized by ethnic Punjabi allied with the Urdu-speaking elite, the rest of the South Asian and the world societies have an unintentional bias towards the social leadership of Sindhi, Balochi, Pashtun and Saraiki origin vis-à-vis those of Punjabi and Urdu origin. This further intensifies issues of high importance and complex nature. The leadership of Punjabi and Urdu origin in Pakistan is well connected with the state, to which they have historically been given agency to participate in decision making. Their input is usually sought after by the establishment in almost all significant internal and external decision making. Besides, they also defend, in numerous cases, even unjustifiable decisions by the state in international forums in an overt or covert manner.

On the other hand, the leadership from Sindh, Balochistan, Khyber Pakhtunkhuwa and Siraiki Southern Punjab has been contributing intellectually to the social and political movements for rights. The journalists, human rights activists, scholars, intellectuals, academicians and literati from these provinces are not only discriminated within Pakistan but also during professional and thematic forums held regionally and internationally.

Similarly, when Baloch or Sindhi journalists, activists and thinkers are persecuted or killed by the state forces, the regional and international media and civil society seldom give them attention. However, when people of Punjabi and Urdu origin from the same professions—which are usually attached to certain layers of the establishment—are victimized, it becomes a matter of concern in regional and international forums.

If the Sindhi or Baloch leadership sympathizes with the political movement of their people and victims of persecution, the world outside criminalizes them. None would even think for the moment that the civil society and media associates and advisors of dominant ethnic groups in Pakistan have also an intellectual share in the crimes against humanity committed by the state. They are generally treated as credible entities. This inability to differentiate between social and civil leadership of the oppressed and the oppressor even by the leadership of other countries is also a kind of bias. Their unwillingness to see perceive both the parties as equals is also a kind of discrimination. It is an exhibition of the people-to-people or civil non-neutrality. This attitude is not only found among individuals but also those in highly reputable rights bodies, media houses, think tanks and intellectuals.

New ethos
A similar problem persists on a lower scale and in different forms when the leadership from the smaller countries, mostly with a single majority ethnic-construct like Nepal, Bangladesh, the Maldives and Bhutan engage and interact with their counterparts from the rest of the developing world. The non-existence of a neutral human interaction and people-to-people contact are more dangerous than that the foreign policies of the establishments of developing countries.

The critical mass of human rights, civil, political and economic justice and peace has grown in the last two decades. This larger tribe of activists, experts, journalists, writers, intellectuals, academicians and other professionals usually identifies itself with the various aspects and levels of social justice. Paradoxically, it lacks justice within its own tribe when it comes to supporting and sympathizing with victims or being neutral when it's a case of the oppressed versus the dominant. This not only applies to broader civil society but also international bodies. A new ethos need to replace old biases, discrimination and non-neutrality, primarily in people's diplomacy.

Published in The Kathmandu Post

MAKING OF TWENTY FIRST CENTURY STATE

States and wars are an outcome of each other. A state has justified legitimacy over the use of violence to maintain peace and order in a justice-oriented manner for the healthy regulation of socio-economic activities. Wars are the history (or 'his-story' in terms of feminism) of our generations. The notion of a peaceful, harmonious, war-free, non-racists, non-extremists and non-chauvinistic world however has to find an appropriate path for the materialization not through the slogans but essentially through the real, practical and pragmatic transformations and reforms within and around the human society, and essentially within the state apparatus of the countries. Juxtaposing to the theoretical aspects of anarchism, the time has not yet come for human society to cede from the institution of the state, because it will ultimately happen through the evolutionary process of transformation in and around the human society and the societal institutions. Therefore, a new world would be impossible without certain sets of reforms within existing state-apparatus in the various human societies. This ultimately would change and re-determine the nature and health of society-state relation and interaction. Unmaking of wars Wars, in the form of feuds, historically were the business of collective communities in the pre-class formation of society. Later on, the warlords of the fiefdoms and tribes undertook this role. Due to industrialization and urbanization of human society on the broader scale, wars became a fundamental characteristic of the early nation-states. Today, war-making is no doubt a sole realm of the state authorities. The decisions of war-making today are taken in accordance with the proclaimed national, regional, continental and international interests. In the political course of contemporary socio-economic history, a twofold set of stakeholders has emerged around the world that have a decisive say in the war-making process - the inter-dependence of weapon and natural resources industry, and narrowly limited states owned think tank groups. The contours of this twofold phenomenon are basically the practices of a no representative process of determining and defining the national interests, and the unsustainable strategies to attain these interests. An unsustainable strategy is a prolonged international engagement in a region or country which does not have appropriate exist strategy; has lesser or no human damages; minimum or no specific impacts on the ecology; and the indigenous population friendly framework. The broader loopholes in the strategic engagements, war-making around the world and unsustainable strategies for attaining interests have given birth today to a kind of global anarchy.

There can be two important aspects of possible global transformation in the context of state-society relations, and particularly with reference to the broader world peace. The world powers and the countries that have heavy-weapon industry may consider the investment and industrial infrastructure transformation to certain extent from weapon industries into soft defense technology so that at least niche of the trade and market demand factors behind the war-making may be minimized. Since the developing countries are gradually becoming self-reliant in the basic heavy weapon industries, which is mostly owned by the states in the developing countries, the weapon industry into the developed world would ultimately shirk in upcoming decades due to natural reduction in the demand. Besides, there is a highly important role of think-tanks in the statecraft, however one should not forget that without certain level of freedom as well as diversity of opinion and schools of thoughts, a think-tank institution or group would be unable to contribute appropriately to the state or the states. Thus, the degree of independence, if not neutrality, of these think-tanks is a prerequisite for the safer world. In fact, a war-free world would only be possible if and when primarily the citizenry of the states and diversity of independent thinking process is also taken into consideration. This becomes a matter of high importance, when it comes to decide as well as define and redefining the national, regional, continental and global interests. Moreover, states should also consider redefining the state-private entrepreneur relationship.

Globalization disparity

The communication revolution and technological transformation has already started changing characteristics of the social classes. The globalization of the socio-political entities including class, technical and intellectual elite or the process of converting sociopolitical, technical and intellectual workers into the globalized elite is an outcome of the contemporary economic-relations and mode productions -- soft, hard, virtual and physical. The current phase of industrialization and steady and voluminous process of urbanization in the world needs to be reflected and thought over through the deep analysis in a manner that a true and real phase of globalization based on the regional and continental parity almost everywhere be initiated. Simultaneously, the globalization disparity among the various sections of a single human society, among the developed and rest of the societies and between the global north and the south needs to taken into analytical consideration so that a more appropriated and healthier process at the planning level may be kicked off. Although this is bound to happen in the certain course of time since the technological and communication revolution would ultimately take human society towards that direction; however states, political groups, media and the social leadership of various nations need to foster the ingredients of the globalization-parity, vertically as well as horizontally, within and among the human societies.

Intellectual dilemma

There is a big difference between the degree and nature of freedom of thought before and after the Second World War. Human societies have no doubt successfully acquired the greater degree of freedom of thought both in terms of rights and collective responsibilities in the post world war scenario. However, the nature of freedoms has shirked, particularly after the mayhem of 9/11. This can be comprehended through the corporate and mainstream media, curbs on social media, state-defined matrix for the most of think-tanks and virtual control mechanisms to resist the freedom of thought. Until nature of the freedom of thought is not redefined around the world, the transformation as well as reformations of the human societies as well as states institutions around the world would be impossible. A new class Over the period of last three decades, the class formation of human society is gradually acquiring the news layers - the social virtuality. It means that although the classical class composition, according to the Marxist interpretation does exist; the new aspects of the classes have emerged due to transformative shift in the mode of production and the technological revolution. Thus, the new class characteristics can also be defined today as the 'virtual elite', 'virtual middle class' and 'virtual poor' for those whose position, influence and nature of work even contradict with their socio-economic realities of the class. It means a poor can also be considered elite if he is powerful in certain social realms more than rest of the poor or middle class person of his / her society or the contemporary poor or middle class person from the other parts of the world.

Creation of new States

The world today is victim of the overall trend of the global statuesque. This situation has caused ecology of international politics in which many a rotten and decades long world issues stands unresolved. The global as well as state level statuesque can be witnessed hitherto from non-resolution of the more than five decades old issues like freedom of Kurdistan, Tibetan autonomy, reconciliation between Tamil and Sinhala in Sri Lanka, and freedom of Sindh and Balochistan from Pakistan. These are the issues that have attracted lesser international consideration and media attention. On the other hand, the issue of the futuristic transformation of Afghanistan is still not appropriately addressed. The recent handover of the training component of Afghan National Army to the Pakistan Army is one such example, which essentially contradicts the principle of healthy transformation of Afghanistan because Pakistan has been the destabilizing and destructive factor for Afghanistan during the ISAF engagement in the war-fatigue land of Afghans. This global as well as state level statuesque has deep roots in the non-representative determining of the national, continental and international interests. It also involves the issues like security at various level; globalization-disparity; the newly emerging virtual identities of 'powerful' and 'weaker' classes; and finally the nature of freedom of media and the individual liberty. Reforms in the international community United Nations (UN) not only needs to be reformed structurally, it also needs to undertake some essential reforms. A real United Nations would only be possible if and when it also forms a tier for the culture and civilizations in the broader fold of the UN in which various cultures that does not qualify the status of nation-states may also get an accredited membership in that United Nation's subordinate layer. This would encourage dying cultures; oppressed societies, social segments; ethno-linguistic groups; and representatives of faiths as well as ideologies to engage with the international community. Besides, the procedures for the International Criminal Court and International Court of Justice needs further to be eased up at the level that crimes against humanity may easily to be taken to the international courts. Moreover, a forum for the federating state also needs to be created in the international body, where the intra-state issues may be addressed without any bloodshed or use of violence. At the same time, a regional, continental and economic level permanent and nonpermanent membership into the United Nations Security Council (UNSC) also needs to be introduced in accordance with the changing world. This will give an opportunity to offer the permanent seats in UNSC for emerging powers like Germany, India, Australia, South Africa and Brazil as well as permanent but non-veto seats of SAARC, ASEAN, Middle East, African Union, and Common Wealth of Independent States (CIS) of exSoviet states as well as Commonwealth of previous British colonies. All these aspects of contemporarily required reforms are inter-dependent. Making a new world would be impossible without making a new state apparatus, and creating a free human society in twenty-first century, where all have their say within the international community forums. *Published in daily Afghanistan Times, Kabul and Merinews, India simultaneously.*

WAVE OF NEW TRANSITION

The recent murder of Indian origin Techie Srinivas Kuchibotls is a violent expression and kick start of what has been bickering up on the backburners of our contemporary times and history. Such socio-psychological developments that led an American to kill young Srinivas have been rooted in the race and ethnicity perspectives not only caused by the globalization but also by the changing economic aspects of today's world.

The Brexit phenomena in United Kingdom (UK) riding on anti-immigration wave; the current such flow in France and some other parts of Europe; and similar incidents exhibiting in Australia is a broader situation with fourfold roots in globalization -- wars and terrorism; changing economic contours of the world; and syndromes caused by increase in the number of non-natives immigrants in the society. It seems the whole upcoming decades of world society would face these challenges.

New Polity and Economy

The centers of international economy and politics today are gradually shifting. Asia is going to assume the role of leading economic power of the world in upcoming one decade. Africa would finally emerge as a new world market in upcoming two decades. The worlds populous most countries, China and India would remain in the club of major economies along with many other economic pockets in Asia. Rise of the regional powers like Germany, India, South Africa, Brazil, Australia and Japan in the world politics would feature the face of polity and economy in the world in upcoming two decades. Northern America and Europe would be pushed to kick off a new kind of polity. Immigration and rise in ethnic-cum-racial nationalism Globalization has given birth to new complexities in the world. It caused high scale immigration towards the West in last three decades. Hundreds of thousands human persons of colored origin immigrated and migrated to the Europe, USA, Canada and Australia. Some amongst them were professionals, other refugees and rest has given shape to a new society across the first world, which is 'white' and is called the West. Ethnicity and race have become the subjects of an entire new discourse in post immigration world of last three decades. Human persons are equal; however according to the United Nations Declaration on the Rights of Indigenous People, indigenous people have special rights over the rest in their territories. This suits best to cases across the world in the continents – Asia, Africa, Europe and South America. USA, Australia and Canada have largest population of no indigenous people. No doubt, native whites and indigenous people of USA, Australia and Canada have their special rights over the rest who have migrated to these lands very recently. The situation has given rise to nationalism based on native ethnicity and race, although religion also seems to be a cross cutting theme of it. This ethnic-cum-race based nationalism is going to dominate the narrative of at least one decade hereafter or a little more. Let the world get prepared about this and seek a path out of such patchy matter.

Muslim Terrorism

Muslim terrorism is a by-product of oil rich Arab countries reaction towards world politics led by the West; wars in some of the Muslim countries; and religious terrorist syndical organism created by the West against Soviets Union during 1970-1980. A tiniest minority sect among Muslims – Salafism is the hardcore of this Muslim terrorism. This today has turned itself a terror syndicalism, which dances to the tunes of hidden hands of some international interests.

Global Society

Amid these new challenges and crises, a new world society has got birth, which is internationalized in its fabric. A human society that is connected with global network of news, human communication, research, analysis, and investment supplemented by the immigrants are the features of today's world society. This has created a new kind of world society --sociology with a bent in the mind. How interwoven are the human persons and human societies today! The ongoing scenario of trends in the West and South America will kick start not only new economy and politics but also an entirely new narrative of policy approach in the countries in the Europe, North America, Australia and South America in ongoing decade that a new chapter in the course of globalization would be written. It would be based on limits to the immigration.

Nations are not going to withdraw their core ethno-racial composite during the course of globalization. Besides, a reaction towards Muslims along with towards the colored people would become more visible in the world we have to see in the upcoming one decade. It is worth mentioning that Canada, Eurasia and Eastern

Europe would be exceptions in this process where relatively healthier socio-psychic tits are expected.

New Transition

This is an era of new transition in human history of our twentieth century. A new fabric as well as narrative of human society is going to be created for us all and by us all that would carve the decades. Upcoming five decades have to depend on upcoming ten years polity, economy and approach in the world. Let us think and act beyond the matrix!

Published in daily Afghanistan Times, and Merinews, India simulteniously.

COMPLEX GLOBAL CHALLENGES

It is a political transition in the world. Phenomenal strategic exceptions are happening simultaneously. A wave of popular protectionism in the West against immigrations; the non-resolution of Afghanistan issue; rising challenge of North Korea and China in the Asia-Pacific, and growing influence and strategic initiatives of China in the world balance of power are the features of this transition. Russia-USA relations adversaries are at the core of the affairs that have helped various factors to take advantage of the situation. In the meantime, threats of Islamic State (IS) and Al-Qaida have become further heightened exhibited in recent terrorism attempts at UK Parliament and failed attempt in the Brussels.

Afghanistan patchwork

US at the moment is focused to its internal affairs. The prolonged Taliban violence in Afghanistan and temporary absence of US from the resolution of Afghanistan stability is eyed by Russia and China to lead the process of negotiations for peace in Afghanistan. A dialogue has been invited over Afghanistan in Moscow for which Taliban have indicated their willingness to participate. With the help of China and through new engagements with Pakistan, Russia would attempt to stabilize Afghanistan by engaging with Taliban. Afghanistan, USA, India and some other countries have remained of opinion that Pakistan has been reason behind Taliban phenomena. Afghanistan officials were quoted as saying that IS emergence in Afghanistan would be handled once Taliban are silenced. IS-Taliban nexus with the help of split groups of Taliban, Al-Qaida and Central Asian terrorist outfits is increasing their activities in Afghanistan and Pakistan. Besides, landlocked

Afghanistan as well as Central Asian countries need nearest route to the sea, which can be availed through either Pakistan or Iran. In any attempt for connecting Afghanistan to the world through sea and causing Afghanistan stability, the world has to choose out of Pakistan or Iran. At the same time, there is a lot to think out of box for the various matters. There are possibilities of USA engagement with Iran through India since India is interested in developing a port in Iran. An Iran-Israel engagement would be another out of box strategic development for the long-term strategic achievement. Pakistan is developing Guwadar and Karachi Ports with support of China through China Pakistan Economic Coordination (CEPEC), which can also connect Afghanistan, Central Asian Countries and Russia with the Indian Ocean although there is Balochistan insurgency and Sindh freedom movement in Pakistan. Terrorism threat is becoming a growing security threat to the world. Their continuous recruitment from Iraq, Syria and other West Asian countries, India, Afghanistan, Pakistan, Bangladesh through the use of modern means of communication have turned this outfit a serious security risk to the world. They have two-pronged strategy – they are fighting guerrilla warfare in Iraq, and using terrorism in Europe, USA, Afghanistan, India and to some extent Pakistan and Bangladesh. Besides, Al-Qaida is silently working on its resurgence according to some reports. This situation really does not need only the security measures and a new approach for collectively addressing this threat but also it requires some fundamental initiatives to alter the thinking matrix among the Muslim population in the world. Hitherto a minority Salafi sect of Islam has been the major school of thought behind violent Muslim expression. Sufi Muslim approach is the only way forward to address this challenge.

Strategic China

China is strategically advancing in so many directions. It is investing in the infrastructure – rails, roads and ports – and business in the Asia, Africa and probably in some parts of the Europe. China is investing $54 billion in Pakistan for CPEC. It is constructing roads and developing Guwadar Port in Pakistan to link Africa and Europe through Arabian Sea and Indian Ocean. It is constructing silk rout to the Central Asian Countries and it is developing a rail track to Nepal. China is also making its strong presence in Indian Ocean. In upcoming decade, China would be strategically present in Asia, Africa and Europe along with a bustling economy. Meanwhile, North Korea is increasing its military and strategic activities aiming South Korea, Japan, and USA. China is also enhancing its presence in the region. Besides, China is trying to induct new members in their economic-strategic alliance of BRICS to counter balance India in the forum and extend its outreach in the world.

Engaging with Russia

In the patchy nexus of strategic and security developments in the world, and slow-paced response from NATO and allies in the context, the situation is further giving agency to various elements to groom. The new situation has been visible after row between Russia, EU and NATO over Crimea. West has to see the things out of box and need to take foresighted steps to create further stability for our generations. An engagement with Russia and Iran as well as other actors offering more cushions is required besides adopting out of box approach to address the strategic challenges that are posed to the world today. Would USA, UK, and EU work together with Russia and some other countries to achieve this? *Published in daily Kathmandi, Nepal*

A WORLD OF SUFISM

Sufism offers a holistic and collective approach to reducing hatred, violence, and terrorism   The world is currently undergoing 'global anarchy'. Human society is witnessing diversified and multiple forms of chaos in the context of human as well as development insecurity. This phenomenon has resulted from the knotty and unsustainable means of strategic manifolds adopted and implemented in the conflict arena during and after the Cold War, especially in today's transitional period of a multi-polarized global balance of power.

The residue caused by the devastations that took place in the socio-political ecology is known today as religious extremism, through which violence as well as terrorism is caused by outfits claiming to be 'Islamists'. Global anarchy and chaos in human society no doubt are new themes of our times, which need a broader and more multi-disciplinary academic and analytical discussion. But at least collective human asset in the form of the 'Sufi' worldview is available. It offers a holistic and collective approach to detoxifying the residues of hatred, and thereby violence and terrorism in the name of religion.

Blending the essence

There are many definitions and meanings of Sufism in the philosophical and theological dictionaries. We will just look at what Sufism is simply, and what exactly it wants. Sufism is an attempt by the spiritual saints and mystic theosophists to explain the existing sprit of humanity within and in the proximity of a religion or among the religions in a non-theologist, non-structural, or semi-structural way. Thus, it is a spiritual as well as spiritual-cum-theosophist path that has the capacity to heal the wounded, misguided, naïve, and perverted human souls to overcome a tilt towards violence or transform them into entirely new spiritual beings.

Sufism, an oriental term, can briefly be defined as a path to clean the inner being of humans. It has many manifestations, expressions, processes, and practices. If geographically categorized, we can see Hindu Sufism, Western Mysticism, and Judeo-Christian Sufism, Oriental, Islamic, South Asian, Central Asian, East Asian, and Sindhi Sufism. Western Sufism has a tilt towards existentialism. Judeo-Christian Sufism is tilted towards the dilution of the finite into the infinite through sacrifice. Islamic Sufism has diversified ways to explain and practice Islam in a sublime way through which a general education of love and inter-dependence is spread among believers of the path. Oriental Sufism has the iconic leadership of Jalal ad-Din Rumi; Islamic Sufisim has the iconic manifestation of Mansoor bin Hilaj and South Asian Sufism is deeply rooted into a path starting from the Vedas and culminating in Guru Nanak. Sindhi Sufism has its foundations in the Rig Veda and a modern outlook in the poetic works of Shah Abdul Latif Bhitai, Sachal Sarmast, and Sami. All these paths and streams within Sufism have one major theme—a balanced and harmonious relationship between and among individual beings, society, and nature, expressed and adopted through spirituality.

Sindhi Sufism is highly peculiar in the broader world of the Sufis. Unlike other streams of Sufism, it mainly attempts to find unity among the diversity of religions. It practices almost all major currents of Sufism into one. A Sufi place in Sindh usually practices Islamic, Hindu, Christian, Judaic, and Buddhist waves of spirituality. This, in theosophy, can only be seen in Baha'ism and its chain of Lotus Temples in the world. Sindhi Sufism has a greater tilt for the existentialist Sufi order, combined with the patriotic Sufi order.

A Sindhi Sufi who is patriotic needs to be a global being in terms of spirituality. Sufism today Alas, there are few academic and institutional works available on and around Sufisim.

The material globalization of the world today and the interfaith-dialogue in human society would be incomplete if it does not offer a broader cushion to Sufism. Sufis have the true spirit to gradually transform human beings from antagonistic into composite human souls.

Published in Daily The Kathmandu Post, Nepal

TEN COMMANDMENTS FOR THE CONTEMPORARY WORLD

Human society needs to adopt new 'Ten Commandments' for the salvation of human beings, the earth, and the life over it. The era of red, green, blue, and saffron tinted ideological states is over. Human society has evolved, throughout the course of its history, some basic values, and principles on which it has repeatedly tried to offer humanity the maximum possible equity, justice, prosperity, and peace. No doubt, however, these values can never be attained in the absolute terms, therefore have always remained relative. The evolution of religions, philosophies, doctrines and sociopolitical theories has always directed to these basic virtues, which is aimed to create new human and thereby a new human society. After thousands years of transcending, the human society once again is at the verge of transcending process for a new order of collective survival, prosperity and liberation in broader terms. It cannot voyage through the time without following seven pliers, which essentially will lead to global justice.

1) All forms of life including human beings have equal right over what is offered by nature on the globe. Human is a higher form of consciousness and is more responsible to the earth and all forms of life over it and on other planets in the universe as well.

2) Rights ensuring human and socioeconomic development that strengthens collectivism and interestedness will lead the individuals and collectives to the social, cultural, and economic liberties and liberations. It requires a new kind of statecraft, political discourse, culture, and development initiatives.

3) Economic self-reliance and livelihood security combined with rights are the foundations of development and human prosperity in the individual societies and around the globe.

4) The people could only achieve the climax of democracy when the theory of 'government by the people' transforms state-society relations into the governance by the people.

5) Justice and Peace are essentials for the human society. If the policies by states, governments, political parties and other social impact making forums are in contradiction with this, they will not only be counterproductive and retrogressive but retaliating as well.

6) Diversity in all of its forms, within the parameters of devised social systems, is a beauty of contemporary human social web and it has emerged on the foundations of modern human and industrial development.

7) An elevated social order is impossible without a necessarily healthier political discourse and culture, which will guaranty social, cultural, and spiritual prosperity. Only spiritually rich and elevated individuals can be the cornerstone of liberated human society. Individual and collective social actions need to be non-violent for the sustenance of human existence.

8) Whatever is offered by nature on the globe as well as in the universe is the collective human property. Individuals have only right on what they humanly produce.

9) Offending nature would retaliate in higher velocity to the human existence. The time has come when all manmade actions need to harmonious with the natural being.

10) Mafias have started dominating the statecraft in the majority nation-states. Revising the role of states and making the nation-states more humanistic is the only path to avoid upcoming global anarchy.

Almost all continents are witnessing anarchy of various forms. The time has come when world needs to sit together on the brewing global anarchy having its deep foundations in the local and global social injustice. Let the construction win over the global soul.

Published on Merinews, India

BLOGS BY THE AUTHOR

INTERVEWS & STORIES BY OTHERS

ANALYTICAL VIEW ON THE BOOK OF ECONOMIC JUSTICE BY THE AUTHOR

OUR DETENTION

It was a summer morning in 2014 when I woke up and found that my upper body was undressed. I along with my wife Fatima were giving a protest demonstration in Delhi and use to sleep those days on a roadside at Jantar Mantar in New Delhi. Someone later that day told us that a gadget (chip) has been inserted in my and my wife Ghulam Fatima's body and my every movement would be recorded. I laughed and said nice joke!

In April 2015, I felt some happening in my body. All of sudden some voices came telling me that they are talking through the chip that is inserted in my body. I was astonished. I did not tell anyone because I felt if I told people would think I have lost my senses. I simply reported this to Connaught Place Police Station. They took me along with them, presented before the Patiala Court judge where I gave my statement. I was made free. The only problem I faced that I was questioned by a Joint Interrogation Team. I slept one night at Connaught Place Police Station.

I was told by someone that was talking through gadget / chip inserted in my body that this is a USA technology. Through this technology people are detained without sending them to the jails and putting them house arrested. A person can live a normal life however his every movement would be recorded. A GPS is part of this technology, which continuously records location of the persons. Whatsoever is talked and seen is also recorded. This technology uses human eyes and ears to record every moment. This gadget works through central nervous system and controls human body functions and organs.

I was told that Pakistan has said to USA that is security threat to Pakistan. USA pressurized India to detain me through this technology hence a chip was inserted in my body while I was in India.

I use to listen through this technology the officials from three countries -- Pakistan (ISI), India (RAW) and USA (CIA). In June 2015, Pakistan authorities started inviting several persons from across Pakistan daily who used to talk about me. They were asked to give political and personal comments. This was continued till January 2017. I listened them.

Through discussion between the officials from the three countries, I learnt that this technology has three components. One is at headquarters in USA; other parts of it are in India and Pakistan.

From April 2016 to July 2016 my body organism was hijacked by Pakistani officials. USA and India officials tried to save my life. Thanks god I survived the murder attempts by Pakistani officials. Once again, my body organs are hijacked by Pakistani (ISI) officials since end of the January 2017. I am continuously being tortured.

Earlier in 2016 during this, in a discussion that is part of the investigations I conducted on certain ISI officials, Pakistani officials have confessed the genocide, rapes and murders in Sindh and Balochistan in an informal discussion between Pakistani participants and Pakistani officials. These confessions are available on the record with India and USA. Pakistani officials also confessed that how they managed the election fraud in Balochistan. Many similar things have been confessed by them.

I was suggested by the doctors that PET scanning is the test through which location of this chip in the body can be identified. Due to scarcity of financial resources, I am unable to undergo that test.

In this situation, an intervention is required to save my life and the life of my wife Fatima. This technology in India is looked after by Deputy Director / Joint Director Ministry of External Affairs India, State Department USA and ISI Islamabad. An engagement with these authorities would save our lives.

AN STORY OF THREE SECURITY IDIOTS AND A MAN FROM MOEN JO DARO

A microchip was inserted in my body by CIA and RAW through the Ministry of External Affairs of India on the request of ISI, Pakistan.

This chip since quite some time leaves damaging impacts on my body organs and organism. This microchip is connected with satellite, and it a neuro-connectivity based technology use it on human brain. It is through human brain, this technology damages human body.

This microchip-based technology does also have mechanism through which the conversation by ISI, RAW and CIA officials reach my ears and I listen. This is continuing since 2015 until now. All such conversations are audio-visually recorded with CIA, RAW and ISI. I am sharing the briefest facts from these conversations, which are officially on the record of India, Pakistan USA.

Previously this Technology was reading my memories to ascertain whether or not is a security threat to Pakistan because ISI claimed in 2012 and later on in 2013 that is a security threat to Pakistan. It was shared with USA, UK, India, Nepal and Afghanistan. The process of reading my memories was completed in the first quarter of 2016. No security risk stuff or moral issue was in my memories. Immediately after completion of the memory reading, another section of ISI took over forcefully and unauthorized control of this Technology and declared their hatred to USA and India.

This technology is owned by USA and in India is authorized for its use in Asia. This news section of ISI also started reading my memories. There were no violent, anti-Pakistan, intelligence agencies related contents in my memories. ISI's claim that is security threat to Pakistan proved untruth. During this ISI asked their district and provincial officials to share their reports regarding   to Islamabad in front of India and USA. They shared their report. According to these reports there was nothing wrong in me. In the meanwhile, MI Pakistan Sindh official also shared with ISI Islamabad that they already have completed the similar investigation regarding which ended in early 2012. Nothing wrong was found in him. Later on, in December 2017 again a senior deputy to Director General of ISI said that nothing is found against, thereafter uttered word "fair" for me. This senior official was a Sindhi. He also gave release orders for me and Fatima for stop using this technology on us. Another section of ISI consisting Punjabi officials along with their seniors refused to obey orders although they were junior to that Sindhi senior officials. On the other hand, ISI also asked around forty thousand persons from Pakistan and outside to come and witness the investigations. Questions were also asked from them regarding us. ISI found everything fine.

In January 2018, ISI Islamabad officials also held an investigation why and Fatima Shah have become victims. The investigation noted that a Pakistan Army working in ISI and was lead officials at ISI Hyderabad basically forwarded an assumption based security note before 2012 for   to the authorities, and caused suspicions in authorities in Pakistan. Therefore ISI conveyed a security note regarding me to above-mentioned countries.

Earlier in mid of 2016, CIA officials told ISI that according to the procedures for using this technology, ISI has to withdraw the use of this technology on Zulfiqar and Fatima through already decided mannerism. CIA and RAW both clearly said that they will not unilaterally stop ISI's use of technology on Zulfiqar and Fatima.

Some ISI officials, although Punjabi Muslims, who ordered torturing us and those also who tortured us through this technology confessed that they were associates and founding fathers of Al-Qaida and ISIS alias Hizbul Ahrar. They also confessed that they ordered 9/11 attacks on USA. Besides, they also confessed that they ordered assassination of Ambassador of UAE in Afghanistan, therefore Taliban attacked UAE Consulate in Qandahar in which   UAE Ambassador and around 20 diplomats and other staff of UAE was killed. They also said they ordered Taliban attack on UAE Consulate individually. When other ISI officials questioned them regarding this, those ISI officials named two previous DG ISI. Their statement regarding them seemed to be contradictory.

Moreover, they also confessed their role in abduction of Sindhi and Baloch activists and thinkers and their murders. They also gave rape orders against Sindhi women to ISI Hyderabad in front of RAW and CIA. They also confessed ordering massacres in Sindh, Balochistan, Khyber Pakhtunkhuwa and of Christian Punjabis in Punjab. One of them said, he declares war on Radhan town of Sindh, which he meant a war on Sindh. One of the Punjabi officials asked his junior to Dewan Industries in Sindh to oust their Sindh laborers. They also said that fake voting was made in Balochistan during 2013 elections.

Later on, these some Punjabi Muslim officials of ISI also disclosed the G.P.S. locations of Pakistani nuclear bombs, nuclear missiles and K.R.L. and Kahota, which are nuclear headquarters of Pakistan. Besides, they also confessed, they have stolen some small nuclear bombs from official storage and want to nuke Kabul in Afghanistan, Gujarat in India and Washington or New York in USA. All this was said in front of CIA and RAW officials.

Furthermore, they also said that a Brigadier General of Pakistan Army working in ISI since quite years in ISI being knew that Osama Bin Laden was present in Abottabad, Pakistan. They also confessed that their team provided security around Osama's Abottabad house. Besides, they confessed that they were behind violence in Iran by the Sunni outfits especially in Sistan-Balochistan and Khurasan provinces. And, they confessed the bomb blast in the Sufi shrine of Qalandar Shahbaz in Sehwan in Sindh as well as a Sufi shrine in Jhil Magsi in Balochistan. They confessed their plan to bomb the shire of Shah Abdul Latif Bhitain and Sachal Sarmast in future. They also confessed masterminding bomb blast in Saint Petersburg in Russia. They said they ordered murder of Chinese citizens in Balochistan.

"I would like to mention and thank USA and India officials that they tried to save my life in 2016. I will also thank some of Sindhi, Baloch, Siraiki, Urdu, Pashtun, Hazara, Kashmiri, Bengali and the few Punjabi officials of ISI those also tried to save my life. Attempts to kill Fatima and me are underway since 2016 through the misuse of this technology. "

Since fathers of Al-Qaida, ISIS and Taliban knew the details of nuclear weapons, and also were in possession of small nuclear bombs, I voluntarily step ahead for peace and nuclear security. I talked in November 2017 with the Defense Attaché at Pakistan Embassy, Paris and Military Attaché desk regarding nuclear security breach by those ISI Islamabad officials. Pakistan Embassy in Paris asked me to engage with these ISI officials and write the details to Pakistan authorities in Islamabad and Rawalpindi. I did this noble work.

In November 2017, Pakistan High Commission in Delhi contacted me. I sent them the letters regarding the nuclear and other confessions by ISI officials, which were meant to be either forwarded to be Pakistan authorities. Prime Minister Nawaz Sharif, chief of armed forces in Pakistan, Pakistan Army Chief, Director General ISI as well as of MI, Secretary Defense and Strategic Defense in Ministry of Defense, Secretary, Ministry of Foreign Affairs, and Intelligence Bureau Pakistan. Thanks to Pakistan High Commission for forwarding these letters to the aforesaid leadership and confirmed this while talking with me on my telephone +918376876614. It was a period of disaster for the world!

In December 2018 a strategic tunnel at Islamabad and the location of nuclear assets in district Qambar Shahdadkot in Sindh came into knowledge to CIA and RAW due follies of a few ISI officials.

"Finally I wrote my last letter to Defense Secretary as well as Military Attaché, Pakistan Embassy, France in Paris along with Pakistan High Commissioner in

India on December 9, 2018 and told them my role regarding above mentioned nuclear security and crises stands concluded. "

It is strange that a portion of Indian system recently behaved with us like ISI persons. Probably do not like Sindhi Muslims from Pakistan. Anyways, I know how to dance with the wolves again and again. Please do not jump to the conclusions. They are not BJP, RSS, Hindutva, Congress and other seculars. They are just mindless persons. Pigmies!

Besides, shah writes, USA has not did a single act for his and his wife's rights. Will the real human rights loving America stand up? He asks Americans. This is just a 'Report to Greeko' – like a novel some of you might have read,.

"Amid dance between life and death, I have also filed two petitions in the International Criminal Court against above mentioned ISI officials regarding ethnic cleansing and genocides in Sindh and Balochistan; exodus of Sindhi Hindus from Pakistan, and use of this technology on us. I have also submitted petitions with Human Rights Council and other forums of United Nations at Geneva. Besides, I have also filed petition in UNOOSA Vienna against the violent use of space technology by these ISI officials on us. I filed petitions with UN Office on Genocide Prevention and Responsibility to Protect at UN New York. Finally, let me know you that we have filed petitions with UNESCO and UN Women. :

I hope these culprits will finally be punished.

ON PAKISTAN DUMPS NUKE WASTE AT SINDH-BALOCH BORDER

By Syed Shihabudheen

Pakistan has been dumping nuclear waste at the Kirthar ranges adjacent to Khuzdar district of Balochistan. Earlier the dumping used to take place in Arabian Sea near and around the Bay of Son Miyani (close to Balochistan coastline) in Lasbela district and parts of Ketch Makran district of the Sindh. This activity poses a grave threat to human life as the dumping sites are not very far from thickly populated areas of both Sindh and Balochistan. Pak authorities have gone to extraordinary length to hide their crime against humanity. First they have taken full control of the mountainous areas that fall in the district Qambar-Shahdadkot, Dadu and Jamshoro. And have denied access to outsiders. Under the Nawaz Sharif regime, the NGOs, both local and international, have lost their voice across Pakistan. Balochistan is no exception. Even those few who are able to operate despite restrictions, are not in a position to conduct medical or other related tests to articulate concerns over N-waste fallout.

Zulfiqar Shah, a Pakistani Sindhi, who has been forced to live in exile has been highlighting the dangers posed by indiscriminate dumping of N-waste by Pakistan government. "I personally authenticate the existence of such hazardous facility in Sindh", he says in a recent blog post. In his assessment, the Nuclear Power House in Karachi that has come up with a Chinese package has always been threatening a mini-Chernobyl kind of carnage for not only the people of Sindhi-Balochistan and nearby India but also for the marine life, biodiversity and Indus Delta Eco-System Shah, who is a prolific writer, has n interesting take on the Balochistan and his native Sindh. In his view both provinces of Pakistan have enough ground to knock at international foray as well as United Nations and The Hague to secure their rights.

"In the elections of 1946 (during the last days of British rule in India), All India Muslim League, which demanded Pakistan, lost the elections in Sindh. Sindhi nationalists formed government in the province in alliance with Indian National Congress. It meant the voters of Sindh rejected the idea of Pakistan, which was created (by the outgoing colonial power Britain) in 1947. This also undid the Pakistan Resolution passed by Sindh Legislative Assembly. Besides, the political leadership and parliamentarians who passed Pakistan Resolution quit All India Muslim League, turned against the idea of Pakistan and won the 1946 elections in Sindh," Zulfiqar Shah wrote on merinews.com this September. He may have his point. More so as he laments that Pakistan Government had jailed the Hur fighters (Sindhi warriors) who had waged war against colonial Britain during the Second World War. Many of these warriors were hanged as well.   may be right that both Sindh and Balochistan have strong valid documentary evidence on their rights. But, it is difficult to buy his view that these two Pakistani provinces should go solo. Now that India has been talking about Balochistan, it will be worth the while to hear Zulfiqar Shah's tale of "stateless life", and the threats he has been "facing" from the dreaded ISI. While in his native Sindh, Shah earned the wrath of Pakistan Army for his civil rights activism, and writings. Closing down The Institute for Social Movements, he was running, he migrated to Nepal in 2012 and UNHCR granted him refugee status. His writings on Pakistan in the Nepali media attracted ISI attention and he became a marked man again. "He was given heavy metal poison by Pakistani intelligence agency, ISI, with the help of its local facilitators" but he survived because of timely medical attention provided by friends. Shah was forced to return to Pakistan in December 2013. Two months later in Feb 2014 he arrived in New Delhi for medical treatment. "He was not only denied appropriate treatment on behalf of Pakistan High Commission, in Delhi, but was also harassed by the high commission officials", says a Wikipedia post. Shah and his wife Fatima staged a protest sit-in for 285 days against Pakistan High Commission and its facilitation by the Indian authorities, the internet posts add. Zulfiqar Shah of Pakistan deserve a helping hand from the governments of the free world and their people. To lead a life of comfort with dignity, wherever they like to live!*Published in a weekly Asia Lite, UK and online on a website.*

LIVING IN EXILE IN INDIA, THIS PAKISTANI COUPLE PRAYS FOR A FREE SINDH AND BALOCHISTAN

By Tarique Anwar, November 02, 2016

Life in exile can only be described by those who experience it. Leaving your motherland is not an easy decision, but people are forced by the circumstances to do so. Zulfiqar Shah and his wife Fatima Siyal Shah is, a Pakistani couple from Dadu district of Sindh province, now stay in a two-room squalid in North West Delhi's Sultanpuri area. No, its not a choice that they made, they were forced to leave their country for raising voice against injustice done to the people. "I wish I could go back to my country but my conscience doesn't allow me. We cannot go back unless Sindh become free or there is political resolution," he told Indiatimes. They say they will not return to their homeland Sindh till it becomes free or there is political resolution. Born in a rural town Radhan in Sindh,   is a civil rights activist, journalist and writer. He has been engaged with the political and democratic rights activism and movements in Sindh since last two decades. He was allegedly forced by the Pakistan Army to leave the country and close down his organization - Institute for Social Movements (ISM), which was playing a leading role in land rights movement in Sindh and Balochistan in May 2012. "Our organization (ISM) initiated a movement against Pakistan Rangers which had occupied the fishing bodies from the fishing communities. The movement ended with then Pakistan President Parvez Musharraf offered apologies on their behalf," he said. This – according to Shah – was the beginning of his troubled times in Pakistan as he was leading that movement. "Since then, I have been under close watch of ISI and Pakistan armed forces," he claimed. But the real trouble for him, Shah said, began when he along with his colleagues raised voice against the "disappearances" of political activists in Sindh and Balochistan at the behest of the Pakistan Army. "In 2007, I joined SAPP (South Asia Partnership Pakistan) and reported about 1,400 disappearances from Sindh and Balochistan in that year alone," he said.

„I was poisoned by the ISI in Nepal" Shah resettled in Nepal where the UNHCR (United Nations High Commissioner for Refugees) had approved him refugee status. In Kathmandu, he started freelancing with the newspapers and websites on the issues of Pakistan particularly concerning Sindh and Balochistan. "I was about to get refugee identity card and refugee travel documents by the UNHCR in January 2013. But, before that, I was given heavy metal poison by Pakistani intelligence agency ISI with local facilitation. However, I was rescued by the local doctors," he said. He was allegedly forced to leave Nepal, thus he left for the country in December 2013. "Five officials of the Pakistan armed forces were secretly accompanying me in the aircarft when I was travelling back," he alleged. Life in exile can only be described by those who experience it. Leaving your motherland is not an easy decision, but people are forced by the circumstances to do so. Zulfiqar Siyal Shah and his wife Fatima Siyal Shah is a Pakistani couple from Dadu district of Sindh province, now stay in a two-room squalid in North West Delhi's Sultanpuri area. No, its not a choice that they made, they were forced to leave their country for raising voice against injustice done to the people. "I wish I could go back to my country but my conscience doesn't allow me. We cannot go back unless Sindh become free or there is political resolution," he told Indiatimes.

They say they will not return to their homeland Sindh till it becomes free or there is political resolution. Born in a rural town Radhan in Sindh, is a civil rights activist, journalist and writer. He has been engaged with the political and democratic rights activism and movements in Sindh since last two decades. He was allegedly forced by the Pakistan Army to leave the country and close down his organization - Institute for Social Movements (ISM), which was playing a leading role in land rights movement in Sindh and Balochistan in May 2012. "Our organization (ISM) initiated a movement against Pakistan Rangers which had occupied the fishing bodies from the fishing communities. The movement ended with then Pakistan President Parvez Musharraf offered apologies on their behalf," he said. This – according to Shah – was the beginning of his troubled times in Pakistan as he was leading that movement. "Since then, I have been under close watch of ISI and Pakistan armed forces," he claimed.*Published in Indiatimes.com*

AWAY FROM HOME, DREAMING OF FREEDOM

ByVishnu Shurma

For this Pakistani refugee couple in Delhi, life is a lonely battle. They long to return, but only if Sindh becomes free, reports Vishnu Sharma By Vishnu Sharma October 24, 2016, Issue 11 Volume 13 For Fatima Siyal Shah, a Pakistani Sindhi refugee in Delhi, her husband is the world. "Often, I wish I could go back to my land but then I look at him and think, what he would do without me," she says. Sitting cross-legged on a borrowed bed and assembled bedding in a small dingy room in Delhi's Sultanpuri, she talks about missing her family in Pakistan but cannot think of going back. "My conscience doesn't allow me to leave him," she says. Fatima and Zulfiqar have been in a self-imposed exile since 2012. In 2013, they came to India on medical visas and have remained here ever since. "When we were coming here for his treatment, I thought it will be all over in a month. I didn't even bring enough clothes," she smiles. Indicating her husband, she says, "Sometimes I tell him I am suffering because of him but then I also understand the pain he is going through." Zulfiqar Shah is a human rights activist and journalist from Sindh who has also worked in several political and community rights organizations. After working in Sindhi language newspapers Daily Kawish and Ibrat, he joined Pakistan's Fisherfolk Forum as Programme Manager. "Our organisation led a movement against Pakistani Rangers who had forcefully occupied the fishing water bodies from the fishing communities," he says. The movement ended after the then president Parvez Musharraf tendered an apology on behalf of the Rangers. However, when Shah started working with South Asia Partnership Pakistan (SAP) his conflict with the Pakistani establishment grew. One of his projects with SAP was on disappearance of political activists in Sindh and Balochistan. "In 2007, we reported 1,400 such disappearances from the two provinces that year alone," he claims. Later, along with his wife and other friends, he founded the Institute for Social Movements, Pakistan. By 2012, his well-wishers in and outside Pakistan convinced Shah that he wasn't safe in the country. He closed down the Institute and fled to Nepal, where he secured refugee status from the United Nations High Commissioner for Refugees (UNHCR). "However, I was poisoned in Kathmandu," he alleges. After initial treatment in Nepal, he returned to Pakistan and applied for an Indian medical visa. On 11 February 2013,

Zulfiqar and Fatima arrived in India. Soon, they realized he wasn't safe here either. "I am sure that I was being watched. I could recognize people even in the restaurants where I went to dine," he claims. According to him, the Pakistan High Commission officials in New Delhi interfered in his treatment too. "I was 'advised' to go back to Pakistan through an AIIMS doctor," he says, showing the 'advice' written on the prescription. When he lost all hope of obtaining assurance for his security in India, he wrote letters to the President, the Prime Minister, the National Human Rights Commission of India and numerous other Indian and international human rights organizations. He also filed a writ petition in the Supreme Court and held a sit-in at Jantar Mantar for nine months demanding resettlement. Later, the government of India granted him long term visa (LTV). "Without LTP we could not open a bank account. We also lost Rs 50,000 in the protest at Jantar Mantar," says Fatima.

According to Shah, Sindh's is the largest and oldest freedom movement in Asia. In March 2014, five million Sindhi people marched in Karachi demanding freedom. "Hardly anybody knows about it. Except Afghan media, no other media has ever tried to highlight the situation in Sindh although Sindh and Balochistan have the largest military concentration in Asia after Iraq and Afghanistan. Does anybody know that after the assassination of Benazir Bhutto on 27 December 2007, Sindh attempted secession from Pakistan?" Like other South Asian regions, Sindh has a multi-layered history, interpretation of which varies. Sindh became a part of British India after the first Anglo-Sindh War in 1843. Thereafter it remained a British protectorate until Independence, after which many wanted Sindh to return to its pre-1843 status. In the early 1970s, the Jeay Sindh Qomi Mahaz was formed and the movement for freedom gained momentum. It is still active. When asked if Prime Minister Modi's mention of Balochistan in the I-Day speech will help, Shah replies, "Of course it will, for Sindh and Balochistan are twins. If Balochistan bleeds, Sindh bleeds too. But it isn't enough. India should talk about Sindh along with Balochistan or Gilgit-Baltistan." Will it not weaken India's policy of non-intervention in internal matters of other countries? "Not at all," responds Shah. "If Pakistan is not hesitant about speaking on Kashmir, which is an artificial issue, why should India shy away from speaking on real issues like Balochistan or Sindh?" he asks. He believes that Sindhi people have been let down by the world, which needs to change its attitude. "The world body has failed to understand Pakistan and its real state construct. It has a dubious and fallacious outlook," he complains.

Today, Fatima feels alone in Delhi. She has no friends to invite on Eid or visit on birthdays. "Mine is a big family. We are six siblings. So, there was always something happening," she recalls. Days pass without the phone ringing even once. From her glassless window, Delhi, looks endless like her own journey. Fatima met Zulfiqar during an interview for a position at SAPP and they fell in love. She had already heard about him from friends in Sindh University. Fatima says that she has more work experience than Zulfiqar. "But ours is a men's world so he jumped the growth ladder fast," she adds. Does she relate with the kind of work her husband is into? "Yes, I do," she asserts. "Sindhis have suffered a lot. Zulfikar Ali Bhutto was our hero and when he was hanged, people of Sindh refused to cook or eat food for several days. After which we wholeheartedly participated in the movement for the restoration of democracy. During the movement, Sindhis were beaten up and even killed. My eight-year-old brother was arrested and kept in confinement for eight days," she says as she wipes her tears. "Later when I started working as a community coordinator I came into contact with people who had gone through similar experiences. With Agha Khan University's Community Health Programme, I did a comparative study on children of different provinces and found that Baloch and Sindh children have nourishment level much lower than children in the rest of Pakistan." Fatima cannot hide her emotions, as she speaks. "Recently, when my elder sister died, I had a fight with him (Zulfiqar). I wanted to fly back home. I had lost my mother at a very young age and my sister was everything to me. I told Zulfiqar to leave me." When she thinks of the future, it seems blank. "I don't know anything about Delhi. I fear what will happen to me if he gets ill. I can't even go out to buy medicines. These days I just can't stop praying." After a pause, she says that she doesn't fear Pakistani authorities any more. "What worse can they do to us? Kill us? But if they kill a human rights defender, what will remain of them?" Do they ever intend to go back to Pakistan, and on what conditions? "Who would not want to return to the land of their forefathers?" responds Shah. "But only on two conditions. One, there is an international guarantee for my life, and two, political reform takes place in Pakistan guaranteeing proportional representation of all ethnic sections. If the latter doesn't happen, soon Pakistan will either dismember into independent countries or there will be a deep anarchy which will engulf the whole of South Asia and afar."

Published Fortnightly Tehlekha, India

IN EXILE IN INDIA, PAKISTAN COUPLE DREAM OF INDEPENDENT SINDH

By Asad Ashraf

Zulfiqar Shah, 39, in his small, dingy room in New Delhi, India, is hoping against hope that Pakistan's Sindh province will be free one day. Living in New Delhi, thousands of kilometers away from his home in Pakistan, life has come to a standstill for him. He has no friends or relatives to visit, no one to socialize with, life for him means waiting for another day to pass. However, through internet, and other means of communication, he keeps himself updated about what's going on in his part of his own country. On being asked if he ever wants to go back to Pakistan, a prompt reply comes, "Not unless Sindh become free or there is political resolution". His wife, Fatima Shah, 50, has worked extensively on the issue of human rights abuses in the Sindh province.

In the isolation of an alien culture in India, Zulfiqar and Fatima mean the world to each other. When in despair they console each other and tell that one day their dream will come true and they will be able to go back to their own free country in their lifetime. "I look at the moon at night and tell myself that people in my part of the world would also be looking at it. The moon becomes a source of consolation for me," she tells WION. She often walks towards the window located in the corner of her dingy room to have a glimpse of an open sky under which both India and Pakistan fall. The couple is living in self-imposed exile in India since 2012. Zulfiqar came here on a medical visa in 2013 and has since decided to stay back. "When we came here, I thought it will be over in a couple of months, I didn't even bring enough items for our survival here," says Fatima. Pointing towards her husband, she says, "Sometimes I feel that I am suffering because of him, but who will understand the pain and suffering Zulfiqar is going through if not me." Zulfiqar is a human rights activist from Sindh in Pakistan, having worked in different newspapers and human rights organizations. After working for two Sindhi language newspapers, he joined the Pakistan Fisherfolk Forum as programmed manager. Explaining his organization's achievement, he tells WION, "Our organisation led a movement against Pakistan Rangers who had occupied the fishing bodies from the fishing communities." The movement ended with then Pakistan president Parvez Musharraf apologizing on behalf of the Rangers. "This was the starting of my troubled times in Pakistan as I was since then kept under close watch on account of the fact that I was spearheading that movement," he claims. But the real trouble for him began when he along with his colleagues acted against the "enforced disappearance" of people in Sindh and Balochistan by Pakistan Army. It was in 2007 that he joined SAPP (South Asia Partnership Pakistan) and reported about 1,400 disappearances from Sindh and Balochistan in that year alone. Later, he went on to form the Institute for Social Movements, Pakistan, with his wife and friends, but had to shut it down later because of threats he received from the government, he alleges.

Zulfiqar had to seek refuge in Nepal after receiving threats to his life for raising his voice for the rights of the Sindhi people and for demanding the secession of Sindh from Pakistan. In Kathmandu he secured refugee status from the United Nations High Commissioner for Refugees (UNHCR). However, he asserts that he was chased by Pakistan's intelligence agency and alleges that he was poisoned by them in Nepal. It was at Nepal's Himal hospital where it was diagnosed that there were elements of thorium present in his body which is generally used by the military. Soon after he left for Pakistan, after getting initial treatment in Nepal. From there he applied for a medical visa for India for treatment at New Delhi's Moolchand Hospital. However, things were not easy for him after reaching India. The couple alleged that he was denied treatment at Moolchand hospital because of pressure from Pakistan agencies. He later went to the All India Institute of Medical Sciences where doctors advised him to go Pakistan as written on his prescription. But it was at New Delhi's Apollo Hospital where Zulfiqar was eventually treated. Zulfiqar said that initially he was being watched very closely in India by ISI officials. He could sense people following him even when he dined out with his wife, virtually forcing him to remain under house arrest. He wrote numerous letters to the Prime Minister of India, President of India and the National Human Rights Commission for their security in the country. "We also filed a writ petition in India's Supreme Court and held a sit-in at Jantar Mantar for nine months. Later, on the intervention of Amnesty International India, the government of India gave us a long-term visa, which we get extended every year," Zulfiqar said.

Zulfiqar is well versed with the history of the region. However, his account of history might differ from the official history taught in Pakistan. According to Shah, Sindh has the oldest freedom movement in Asia and like other South Asian regions, has a multilayered history with different interpretations. After the first Anglo-Sindh war in 1843, Sindh became a part of British India and remained a British protectorate until independence. Following which a majority of the Sindhis wanted to return to the pre1843 status. Jeay Sindh Qomi Mahaz was formed in the early 1970s for demanding freedom from Pakistan. The movement is still alive, he says. He reveals that there have been three marches so far where Sindhis have time and again raised the demand for freedom from Pakistan.

In March 2014, five million Sindhi people marched in Karachi demanding freedom from Pakistan. But such movements have largely been ignored by the international media. Except for the Afghan media, no other media has tried to depict the plight of the people of Sindh and Balochistan, which has the largest military presence apart from Iraq and Afghanistan. "Does anyone know that Sindh had seceded from Pakistan for three days after the assassination of Benazir Bhutto in December 2007?" he asks. Stressing on the sovereignty of Sindh, he says that Sindhi language has been recognized by India's Parliament and also the US Parliament, indicating that Sindh is a separate sovereign nation. Referring to the last letter written by former Pakistan prime minister Zulfiqar Ali Bhutto to his daughter, Benazir Bhutto, he says that the leader had mentioned that Sindh would say 'Khuda Hafiz' to Pakistan before Balochistan. When asked about Prime Minister Modi's reference to Balochistan in his Independence day speech, he says, "It will help Sindh too since Balochistan and Sindh are twins, and if one bleeds, the other bleeds as well. However, he asserts that Modi should also specifically talk about Sindh, which would bring forth the plight of Sindhis to the world. Asked if India's interference in the internal matters of Pakistan will affect the nonintervention policy of India, he had this to say, "Not at all, when Pakistan can talk about Kashmir, why can't India talk about Sindh and Balochistan which largely remain neglected by the world." However, such strong political commitment does not come easy for the couple who in their struggle have lost everything and everyone. India is a not a home for them and they are living here as refugees.

Fatima tells WION, "I used to often break down, but Zulfiqar gave me strength. He consoled me and gave me the courage to fight all the odds in a bid to secure our rights. After all, big leaders across the world had to flee their countries and live in exile." "I relate to the kind of work my husband does. Sindhis have suffered a lot in Pakistan. Zulfiqar Ali Bhutto was our hero. When they hanged him, the entire Sindh mourned. We participated in the movement for restoration of democracy in Pakistan. Sindhis were beaten up and assaulted then. My brother, who was just eight years old, was arrested and kept in confinement," she adds. Unable to hide her emotions, she breaks down while talking about the death of her elder sister. "I could not attend the last rites," she says.

On a lighter note, Fatima says that she has more work experience than Zulfiqar, but he is more famous as it is a male-dominated world. The future seems bleak for her in Delhi. "I don't know what will happen to me if something happens to Zulfiqar. Where will I go, I have nobody here. But I left everything on God. Let him do justice for us," she says. On being asked if they would be again going back to Pakistan, Zulfiqar responds, "Who would not want to go back to the land where he belongs, but not until till there is an international guarantee for my life, and two political reforms take place in Pakistan, which means ensuring equal rights and representation for all the ethnic communities living in the country." "If the latter does not happen, Pakistan will crumble into small pieces," he adds. Responding to his sufferings here in India, he says, "It's better to suffer than to live an undignified life in Pakistan. For me, Sindh is above everything else." *Published on WION*

"LINE OF WEALTH": WHY LINE OF WEALTH THEORY IN ECONOMY WILL REPLACE THE SOCIALISM AND CAPITALISM TOGETHER

Scholar, ideologue and economist Roshan Lal Agrawal has authored a new doctrine in the economics, which is Line of Wealth. This has published in English language book "Line of Wealth". In fact his original work is in Hindi, "Gharibi Rekha Naheen, Amiri Rekha". The doctrine in the book is a new addition in the disciplines of economics including development economics, fiscal economy and taxation. This book, in fact, is the important most treatises after Karl Marx and Engels doctrine of socialism. The book is an expression in a simple yet academic style and manner. This is the chapter wise review, pricy and commentary on the book, which also includes some excerpts as well.

Chapter 1: Desire of Peace

Science has changed the life styles and mode of business as well as commerce through modern technology inventions. Inventions in physics mainly communication revolution, robotics and transportation has entirely changed the active life, living patterns, and professions. Today, the capacity of production has increased and inversely the large number of laborers have become unemployed because technology has steady replaced the human labor. Contrarily, the opportunities to accumulate the wealth by a few have increased. Until this inequality and contradiction is not solved, peace in broader terms cannot be achieved.

Chapter 2: Survival

Human require consumables for life. The inequality begins with the competition not only on the optimum requirements for consumables for everyone but also to save them. Saving of consumables, in the beginning, started for future troubled times however this laid foundations for accumulation of consumables which later on grown as accumulation of wealth. This has caused extreme poverty. Majority in the world cannot afford the food, clothing and shelter. This human socio-economic process has been main reason behind strife and wars.

Chapter 3: Economic Justice

Economic justice is when freedom and equality in terms of economy are give to all, which in turn will strengthen the freedom and equality in other spheres of society. Economic justice is basically three pronged: equal rights of all on natural resources, public audit and payout on the wealth accumulation beyond certain limit and equality amongst all haves and have-nots as well as post scientific revolution situation equal economic opportunities for all. In the absences of economic justice, slavery, unemployment, crime and violence cannot end.

Chapter 4: Line of Wealth

Majority in the world is wealthless. "In order to establish justice, all aspects of socio-political economy need to be rethought. Justice is all citizens have equal rights on natural resources of a country. Human persons have this right since the birth," writes author. In a bid to attain and establish economic justice, an approach change is required. World has to withdraw much touted approach – the Line of Poverty. Instead, it requires the approach Line of Wealth. Line of Wealth is simply putting a ceiling on the per capita possession of wealth that should be declared one's fundamental right and go untaxed. The wealth more than the ceiling of wealth possession should be heavily taxed, meanwhile all other domestic taxes should be abolished. Thereafter, the revenues generated due to wealth tax, which the author has termed 'national income' should be utilized for the government requirement, while the remaining revenues or net saving should equally distributed among the citizens.

Chapter 5: An Ideal Economy

"An ideal economy is when all means of production together meet the needs of people," is the one sentence definition of an ideal economy by the author. The 'surplus resources' as author has termed the impacts on the available natural due to human purists for the accumulation of wealth, which in fact is unsustainable and is bound to reduces opportunities for the upcoming generation for their economic wellbeing. Author is of the view that there should be cycle of wealth flow in all classes, sections and strata of society, which in result will ensure the sustainable and collective outcomes for economy in general and for all.

Chapter 6: End the Scarcity

Natural resources are scarce if seen the growing population of the world, and the scenario is further worst if viewed in the futuristic or next generations' perspective. This further impulse to develop a new economic matrix for checking scarcity in sustainable manner both for the world today as well as for the upcoming generation. Therefore, the only way out to check or sustainably and permanently end the scarcity is to adopt the approach of putting ceiling on the wealth possession, and the wealth beyond that ceiling should be taxed heavily. No other tax domestically imposed. Putting ceiling on the possession of wealth along with introducing one-tax system based on taxing wealth more than the ceiling is two major aspects of the Line of Wealth approach doctrine by Roshan Lal Agrawal in his book, "Line of Wealth". Besides ending scarcity, it will also end the tax burden on citizens, minimize inflation possibilities, end corruption, governance expenditure reduction, financial management and related expenditure reduction both in public and private sectors, permanent and sustainable end to unemployment and poverty, reduce population pressure on cities, benefit agriculture and industry laborers, ensure old age benefits for all, end the need for artificial injecting financial resources into various sectors.

Chapter 7: One-Tax System, National Income and Economic Equality

The new taxation regime of one-tax system levied on the wealth exceeding the ceiling called Line of Wealth will generate extraordinary more revenues than the existing revenue generation of the countries is. These revenue is termed by the author as "national income" In the sample analysis of India, the author of the book proves through official and estimated independent data that after meeting government expenditures in India, and spending more on the other needs of the country and the people, the net saving if multiplied with the population of India, each citizen will receive INR 10000 monthly as royalty of their right to natural resources in the country. After this all, the surplus funds can be utilized to make India debt free.

Chapter 8: Wealth, Family, and State

According to author, a family consensually selects a representative of the family to the institutions of state, whenever a family or the state system wants to engage with a family. Progressively, he suggests that an outsider can also be a member of a family through the consensus of the family. Such new family member's wealth, if one does have, will be considered wealth of that family, and if someone does not have wealth, he or she will be having rights to the wealth of the family or at least of the family member who gives proposal for making someone member of the family. He also emphasis that each family unit in a country should be registered with the government. Besides, he also focus the drawbacks of wealth confidentiality law in India, like everywhere in the world, and clearly concludes ending assets or wealth confidentiality law, which cause tax evasion, corruption and malpractices. He is of the view that a citizen should be given right to assess value of his own immoveable property, pay taxes according to that and sale of that property should also be in accordance with that through a property sale mechanism which he also suggests in the book. On those bases, he also suggests the property sale registration revenue methods. He also narrates the requirement of implementing the ceiling on the wealth, and thereby implementation of taxation on the more than that ceiling or line of wealth one possesses.

Chapter 9: A Free World

Globalization has manifestations and connotations. It is a globalization of the industry, trade, commerce, connectivity of people for business, professional and personal matters, which has reduced time and cost in all these areas. At the same time, there is also globalization of crime, terrorism and violence. Besides, the global wealth and wealthy interests have started highly influencing electoral sovereignty of the countries; therefore, such vested globalized wealth interest in various cases has also been factors behind the election victory of the parties to form government in a bid to facilitate such wealth interests. How maintains that economic justice vision is the only path to get rid from such kinds of negative aspects of globalization.

Chapter 10: On Social Disorder

The reason behind the social disorder in the society is economic, the accumulation of wealth. According to the author, "consumption" is the central reason behind the accumulation of wealth. Since the natural resources are the actual wealth, all other forms of wealth are manifestation of it; therefore, the basic reason of social disorder is the natural resources and its unjust distribution, possession and accumulation.

Chapter 11: Purpose of Economy and Importance of Justice

According to author of the book, "the fundamental purpose of the economy is to provide consumables in abundances to meet consumption requirement and avert scarcity of consumable ... in a bid to avoid scarcity, human has developed science, art, structure and process of economy." Besides, the author further writes, "contrary to the fundamentals of a cross-sectional social order, the possession and control of production and market by a few ... [has caused] unjust distribution of the (benefits) in the society (because of) modern developments in the technology, production, and market." The author has touched deeply as aspect of basic right of human on natural resources, which is the invisible relation of human, exclusively the laborer, with the natural resources through the physical existence of the modern technology – the very much tools. Hence, the author in the book has extensively elaborated and proved that his theory of equal right on the natural resources is the actually hitherto almost untouched unearthing of the economics blended with sociology aspect.

Chapter 12: Exploitation Free Market System

Market is practically determining factor behind the prices of the production for the sale and purchase; however, the producer is the basic price determining entity. The author favors the open market; however, he is against the hoarding, extraordinary price hike due to monopoly and hoarding together. He also suggests mechanisms and system to end malpractices free market that according to author is free for all – the producer, seller and buyer together. In fact, he talks about a playing field level for all these stakeholders. Besides, he also suggests education for above-mentioned stakeholders with reference to free market process.

Chapter 13: Fair Economy: A Review of Existing Ideologies

Author opines on the Capitalism and Socialism practiced in the world after Soviet revolution led by Lenin in the Soviet Union. According to the author socialism controls all modes of production by nationalizing them on the argument since they are representatives of poor, therefore they take control of mode of production on behalf of poor; however the author disagree and criticize the socialist practices of restricting human freedom, and creation of new classes of powerful and powerless due to one party rule and bureaucracy, which according to him caused limits to economic progress; hence economic and political justices did not exist there resultantly caused collapse of socialist system in the world. On Capitalism, his criticism is in contrast to socialism, capitalism gives freedoms to individuals however does not gives freedom and equality in the field of economics. Author also writes that Socialism was unavoidable alternatives of Capitalism and relatively was pro poor. However author's theory in this context is the despite classless society, a class barer free society or a class free society is the only path in which freedoms and equality together be ensured to all. Author sees Line of Wealth approach based ceiling on the possession of private property despite abolition of private the only economic justice in today's world, this according to author combined with the equal rights of all on the natural resources in a country is the contemporary doctrine to create a class free society. The way word 'socialism' author has used in his book does mean the practices by the claimant to be Socialist countries led by Communist Parties. So far ideological perspectives, he is against the typical the last century's practices in the name of Preliterate Dictatorship as well as Abolition of Private Property. He, despite, sees rich and poor equal in the humanity. He writes for both equal rights on the mode of productions and natural resources; however he theorize the model of one-tax system to heavily tax rich and distribute these taxes as Dividends among all citizens equally only to those who possess wealth bellow the Line of Wealth. Besides, he believes modern democracy is the real democracy if the economy in country is based on the authors' doctrine economic justice. Therefore, author despite favoring unelected Proletariat Dictatorship, favors elected political leadership and democratic governance. His doctrine of revolution is basically based on the revolution in the economy through electoral process implement ceiling on the possession of wealth, and the revenues through taxing wealth more than that ceiling to be considered a collective property which author terms 'national income' and suggests after governance expenditure, all remaining revenues to be distributed equally among those who either possess wealth bellow the ceiling or does not possess. In fact his model of revolution is through fiscal and taxation regime change.

It is important to mention here that although Socialist revolution was brought by V. I. Lenin and Leon Trotsky together in which Trotsky was Commander (Commissar) of Red Army which took hold of tsar's Russia through war, and after revolution Lenin led the country as Union of Soviet Socialist Republic. Immediately after that revolution, which popularly is known as October Revolution, Lenin died due to brain hemorrhage. Trotsky was ousted from Soviet Union due his notions and labeled as traitor of the revolution; meanwhile other members of Polit-Bureau of Bolshevik Party (Communist Party – Revolutionary) were found assassinated. The only remaining leader out of the Polit Bureau of Bolshvik Party that did evolution was Stalin, who led the country and gave the socialist system, mechanism and method, therefore the socialist in Soviet Union and in the rest country's of the world was Stalanism, neither Marxism, nor Leninism and Trotskyism. Therefore the word 'Socialism' in this books considered Stalinist model of socialist state and society practiced in the world, later n failed to continue. Thus, the collapse and fall of Soviet Union and other socialist countries was not failure or defeat of Maxism-Lenenism-Trotskyim, it was failure and defeat of Stalinsim only.

Chapter 14: Impacts of Contemporary Economy on Environment

"Any production which cannot be used for consumption has no importance...," writes the author. When producer produce more than sellable production, in other words, more than purchasing power, which according to author a production with not consumption, is usually burned by the producer. Such act of discarding the commodities cause environmental degradation, therefore, author writes that economic justice vision is the only way out to avoid such anti-environment acts by the producers both industrialist and agriculture investors.

Chapter 15: Taxation in India, Ethics and Social Transformation

According to the author, "the legal, procedural and structural drawbacks of existing taxation system cause black-money, corruption and inflation." The author opines that existing taxation system in India is unjust, based on the favors to the wealthy. Its procedures lead to fallacious taxation including tax theft. It also leads citizens to provide inaccurate data and details while undergoing taxation process. It mentions that structural and process expenditures of tax collection in India are extra ordinary high therefore; the net revenues level is skewed. The author pens that taxation system even sells the property of a persons who is unable to pay the taxes due to exceptional health or similar emergency or unforeseen expenditures. The author talks on the taxation regime change in India. It professes the implementation of one-tax system on the wealth above the ceiling decided for the wealth possession –I-e Line of Wealth. This, according to the author, will save system costs of the taxation process and structure by highly reducing the taxation department (s) as well as simplifying the taxation procedures. Besides, he writes that the one-tax system will ensure that no un-taxable in pure fiscal terms or fiscal-ethics terms will be taxed. Besides, author writes that one-tax system will generate more revenue in comparison of revenues generated by current taxation process and procedure.

Chapter 16: Origin and Ownership of Interest

Author terms interests in the academic expression "the interest can be said a kind of opportunity cost, which lender takes from the borrower." The author is of the opinion since the business entrepreneur mostly takes loan on the interest, and includes the interest on the loan in the price of commodity; therefore, consumers pay the interest on the loan it borrows. Therefore, the interest on the loan should also be considered public property and should have a mechanism to distribute fairly among all stakeholders.

Chapter 17: Private Wealth Rights

Author writes that all the citizens of a country have unalienable fundamental equal rights on the natural resources. Besides, author elaborates the why the ceiling on the possession of wealth is required in the contemporary economy. The author writes that wealth in any of its forms, if exceeds the ceiling on the wealth possession, should be heavily taxed, and this one-tax should be levied. All the other existing tax should be abolished. While writing this, author regarding fiscal aspects of economic justice, only talks and sees the things in the book and in whole of his ideology only in the perspective Gross Domestic Production (GDP). It has not penned in the book, the aspects Gross National Production (GNP) both in terms of wealth possession, import-export and other aspects of GNP. Therefore, the fiscal regime change, which author calls one-tax system and national revenues, is based on only fundamental and larger part of the economy of a country; however in the reality of globalization of trade and commerce, a GNP as well as global economy perspective doctrine on the economic justice. This needs to be expressed as well.

Chapter 19: State, Politics & Minimal Government

What exactly the democracy is? Is vote right and electing a government and the parliamentarians and others enough to accomplish or claim a system democracy. An essential democracy is when economic democracy already exists in the society. In a society that already have economic democracy, a voter votes properly. The very much economic democracy combined with political democracy is economic justice provided that inalienable equal right to natural resources is given to all. When equal taxation system will be implemented in a country, based on one-tax system – heavy tax on wealth one possesses beyond the certain limit – the size of government will reduce and a minimal government will properly provide governance to the people.

Chapter 20: Questions & Answers on Economic Justice

Common, touchy and ifs as well as buts by the people are replied in simple language in a bid to further make the vision of economic justice understandable.

A COSMIC VIEW OF THE BOOK AND DOCTRINE "LINE OF WEALTH"

Recently published book, "Line of Wealth" by popular economist and scholar Roshan Lal Agrawal is an economic treatise in which his theory around "consumables" is one-step forward in comparison with existing theories of economics. Until now, the economic narrative has been around the comedies and production, which set the dictum of market, finance and other sectors of the economy. The 'consumable' context and reality of commodities, productions and services is a beginning for a paradigm shift in the trade, commerce, agriculture and industrial economy – both in theory and in practice. If simply seen, his doctrine has following basis:

Fundamentality of consumables as bases for casual results in the economic process of production, consumption, monitory circulation, accumulation of wealth, net use of labor as essential factor in the determination of price of production; market; surplus wealth, surplus labor and in-sustainability in the pursuits of economic growth; fiscal disparity, injustice, procedures and malpractices.

The Agrawal doctrine if compared with re-distribution of wealth, which politically is one of the responsibilities of state system and policies, is a post-redistribution of wealth theory in his whole doctrine composite, which can be said the re-distribution of wealth based on economic justice with foundations in the Line of Wealth approach. He like Karl Marx, has upside down the theory of redistribution of wealth in the economics, and unlike Marx has focused on surplus wealth, thus a new, simple and expressed in popular academic language has originally given a theory that can be said Das Wealth, not Das Capital, in the post Soviet collapse world of global economy. Therefore the book, 'Line of Wealth' can actual be called

Das Wealth, which is a Southasian view of seeing at the economic phenomenon. He focuses wealth as such, not like Marx, the Capital part of the Wealth. Despite focusing classes, he has focused wealthy and wreathless, therefore he doctrines the interweaving the classes together in which pens agency for wreathless in the wealth of wealthy, and at the same time he also recognize the wealth ownership right of the wealthy. The agency of wreathless in the wealth of the wealthy is rent payment of the excessive wealth ownership to the wreathless citizens in a country that are the real owners of a countries everything. Agrwal calls it people's royalty in the wealth that one possesses more that certain limits.

Simplicity of the style and narration of the book is also in his concepts. He calls this rent or royalty payable to the citizen, Citizen's Tax (Nagrik Bhatta in Hindi) on the excessive wealth. He professes levying only one tax -- the heavy tax on excessive wealth -- and theories the abolishment of all other taxes. Again, he claims that wealthy will not be antagonized by such taxation. Because, according to him if a wealthy pays heavy one tax, he at the same time will not pay other taxes, and will save the financial cost as well.

What Agrawal has not mentioned in the book is the reality that the industrialists and service providers will not collect the General Sales Tax on the production, therefore cost of the financial infrastructure and expenditure for such taxed GST and other duties that are to be sent to the governments will be saved. Meanwhile, the other financial expenditure will also reduce. The reduction in the cost will lower the prices of the commodities which will serve the consumers, sellers and producers because the productions will fall in the purchasing power of the low income group as well, which in turn cause more quantity of production due to increase in the demand and in final result the investor, the market persons and the consumers together will get benefits. More interesting this whole again will create new persons that will come in the ambit of wealth tax and the whole cycle of new taxation will create a new economic, financial, fiscal and market arrangements.

Agrawal's book in general talks of one tax however; he also talks of the two other taxes regarding the ownership of immoveable property, its sale and sale mechanism. Agrawal's approach towards estate property ownership is more focused on market and pens for turning concerned government department to become a market-oriented entity with the system.

At one point, he becomes an idealist and pens something absurd – the determination of cost of a commodity or production on the basis of labor utilized for it. This is the point, where Agrawal does not mentions that cost an investor pays to the labor as wages as well as contracts of laboring, which is already included in the cost of the commodities in the market. It is hope Agrawal will write next book to elaborate this aspects of his theory. Whether he wants wage-labor should be paid high, and thereby cost of a commodity be determined on the labor cost? This will cause price hike, and shirk the consumers' capacity to purchase. Let Agrwal write on the labor as such. I am of the view that an accumulative quantum of the labor used in each process of manufacturing, service and production is considered as labor used per se, and thereby the price of the commodities be determined. The pricing commodities with cost perspective as well as labor perspective are different; and create a complete upside down in the macro and micro economics in the courtiers and the in global economy. This is already practiced in the software industry whose commodities and services are priced on the basis of quality labor used; however excluding expenditure factor from pricing and solely being based on utilized labor even in thought of he accumulated labor utilized in a production will be an other kind of economic injustice. In anyway, everything has to have economic value – labor or love. Therefore, ultimately again economic value of accumulated labor used will be valued in economic terms, which has monitory face. Therefore, a Das Labor is required in Agarwal's opinion in his schema, which will be a new in fact Darwinhood in the world economy. A modern Marxism will in fact get birth.

Besides, Agrawal should also write on the two aspects of the commodity and its price determination: (a) the import and other similar taxes on the raw, parts and semi-manufactured final commodities in the context of wealth, and (b) its use as cost factor for price determination of a commodity.

What Agrawal has not written is the use of cheap labor from developing and underdeveloped world for the manufacturing and services. The industrialists must be taxed at least moderately for acquiring cheap labor, and ensuring distribution of it among those cheap labor although it is a reality that high population countries like China and India have become beneficiaries for creating the new employment opportunities for their unemployed citizens. Why not an import taxes free economy be part of Agrawal's doctrine to further agree the wealthy for one-tax on the wealth? This will also lead the protectionist economic approach to end, and will create a fiscal globalization in the world. This will kick off the process of globalization for the poor and labor. Besides, achieving the goal of development through tax free imports in a country, the attraction for industrialists for that economy will increase which will cause new industrial and urban societies in the world – provided that this is done as part of Agrawal's Line of Wealth doctrine, which ensure surplus financial resources for the governance only through domestic taxes and discuss around GDP of a country.

The foundation of justice is equality.

In the human justice, the meaning of Economic Justice is a situation where every human being has equal share on the natural resources. It is not based on the talent, aptitude or effort. It is just beyond that. Economic justice is a fundamental human right, and cannot be violated.

On the foothold of this rights regime, a person's right on the wealth can tangibly be measured in a ceiling on the wealth that fall in the fundamental right sphere. The possession of wealth more than the ceiling should be considered outside the fundamental right. This ceiling on the wealth is the average Line of Wealth, and simply can be called average right on the wealth. Any other unequal rights, possession or ownership on the natural resource is injustice.

What Agrawal has not mentioned is the pink revolution or red-reforms by comrade Hyder Bux Jatoi in Sindh's rural economy and peasants, landholders, the agriculture related business and laboring. He simply led the movement of peasants; succeed in the legislation of Sindh Tenancy Act in 1950s according to which owner of arable land will receive half of the crop production as rent of his land; however land owners spends the larger part on the inputs for the cultivation, therefore a peasant gets half of the crop produce as seasonal wage of his labor. Besides, a peasant can use the woods and grass for the cattle without paying to the landowner. Besides, if a peasant is homeless, and there is piece of uncultivated land nearby, his family can built a home and become owner of it without any cost. According to Sindh Tenancy Act no land owner can evict the peasant, if this happens there is a First Class Magistrate's Court for the resolution of the matter. Besides, if a landowner use abusive language to the peasant, he will become liable to fine. Importantly, if land owner sales his land, the first right to purchase that land is given to the peasant. This changed the sharecropping in Sindh, which immediately after adopted by the rest provinces in Pakistan. In fact, ceiling on the land ownership by Nehru is already practiced in India in which arable land more than the ceiling was confiscated from the landowners and distributed among the landless peasants. In fact, Jatoi reforms in Sindh and rest Pakistan were materialized much before the Nehru did. Such reforms prevented from Maoist revolution in Pakistan. Unlike Nehru, Agrwal doctrine is against the confiscation of wealth in all forms; despite it talks about new taxation system in which a Citizen's tax be levied from those who possess more than the ceiling of the wealth through one-tax system. His predecessor is Hyder Bux Jatio, who started people's movement before partition of Subcontinent in peasants and arable landowner context in which he termed landowner as legitimate to receive rent of land toiled by the peasants as well as invest in the crop production for receiving half of the crop produce. If seen in Agrawal's doctrine, Jatoi became successful to implement Peasant Tax like thing in Pakistan. Jatoi launched this movement of peasants in camaraderie with Jamshed Nasrawan Ji Mehta and G. M. Syyed.

The exclusive most aspects of Agarwal doctrine are Line of Wealth approach, the new fiscal policy and taxation regime, and unalienable equal right to natural resources of citizens in a country or a land.

LINE OF REFORMS AND "LINE OF WEALTH"

The book, "Line of Wealth" (Garibi Rekha Naheen, Amiri Rekha – in Hindi) by economist and scholar Roshan Lal Agrawal is an economic treatise in which his theory around "consumables" is one-step forward in comparison with existing theories of economics. Until now, the economic narrative has been around the comedies and production, which set the dictum of market, finance and other sectors of the economy. The 'consumable' context and reality of commodities, productions and services is a beginning for a paradigm shift in the trade, commerce, agriculture and industrial economy – both in theory and in practice. If simply seen, his doctrine has following basis:

Fundamentality of "consumables" as bases for casual results in the economic process of production, consumption, monitory circulation, accumulation of wealth, net use of labor as essential factor in the determination of price of production; market; surplus wealth, surplus labor and unsustainability in the pursuits of economic growth; fiscal disparity, injustice, procedures and malpractices.

The Agrawal doctrine if compared with re-distribution of wealth, which politically is one of the responsibilities of state system and policies, is a post-redistribution of wealth theory in his whole doctrine schema, which can be said the re-distribution of wealth based on economic justice with foundations in the Line of Wealth approach. He like Karl Marx, has upside down the theory of redistribution of wealth in the economics, and unlike Marx has focused on surplus wealth, thus a new, simple and expressed in popular academic language has originally given a theory that can be said Das Wealth, not Das Capital, in the post Soviet collapse world of global economy. Therefore the book, 'Line of Wealth' can actual be called Das Wealth, which is a Southasian view of seeing at the economic phenomenon. He focuses wealth as such, not like Marx, the Capital part of the Wealth. Despite focusing classes, he has focused wealthy and wreathless, therefore he doctrines the interweaving the classes together in which he pens agency for wreathless in the wealth of wealthy, and at the same time he also recognize the wealth ownership right of the wealthy. The agency of wealthless in the wealth of a wealthy is the rent payment of the excessive wealth ownership, which has to be paid to the wealthless citizens in a country. In fact, the citizens are real owners of a countries everything. Agrawal calls it people's royalty in the wealth that one possesses more that certain limits.

Simplicity of the style and narration of the book is also found in his concepts. Agrwal schema of economic justice is not a complex structure of theories. It is very simple and based on the universal truth as have proven hitherto. He translated one of the foundations of his doctrine schema -- every citizen's equal right over natural resources -- into the structural part of his schema for establishing economic justice. Thus, he in the context of fiscal aspect of economic justice, calls natural resources right a Citizens' tax or people's royalty on the wealth that exceeds the ceiling of the un-taxable wealth in a country. This in Agrwal's word is 'rent' or 'royalty' 'payable to the citizen'.

He professes levying only one tax -- a heavy tax on excessive wealth -- and theorize the abolishment of all other taxes. Again, he claims that wealthy will not be antagonized by such taxation. Because, according to him if a wealthy pays heavy one tax, he at the same time will not pay other taxes, and will save the financial costs as well so far financial management is concerned.

What Agrawal has not mentioned in the book is the reality that the industrialists and service providers will not collect the General Sales Tax on the production, therefore cost of the financial infrastructure and expenditure for such taxed GST and other duties that are to be sent to the governments will be saved. Meanwhile, the other financial expenditure will also reduce. The reduction in the cost will lower the prices of the commodities. It will serve the consumers, sellers and producers because the productions will include into the purchasing power of the low income group as well, which in turn cause more quantity of production due to increase in the demand and in final result the investor, the market persons and the consumers together will get benefits. More interesting this whole again will create new wealth persons that will come in the ambit of wealth tax and the whole cycle of new taxation will create a new economic, financial, fiscal and market arrangements ecology.

Agrawal's book in general talks of one tax however; he also talks of the two other taxes out of which one is regarding the ownership of immoveable property, its sale and sale mechanism. Some new fiscal parameters for the stamp duty as well as ownership transfer fees also part of fiscal aspects of materialization of economic justice in Agrawal schema. Agrawal's approach towards estate property ownership is more focused on market and pens for turning concerned government department to become a market-oriented entity within the government system regarding economic valuation as well as sale mechanism of the immovable property.

At one point, he becomes an idealist and pens something absurd – the determination of cost of a commodity or production on the basis of labor utilized for that. This is the point, where Agrawal does not mention that cost an investor pays to the labor as wage as well as contracts of laboring, which is already included in the cost of the commodities in the market. It is hope Agrawal will write next book to elaborate this aspects of his theory, which is detached attachment of his Schema. Basically it is a notion by him, which he has not elaborated. If he wants higher wages for laborer, it will increase cost of the commodities whether or not the price is determined based on labor utilized. This will cause price hike, and shirk the consumers' capacity to purchase. Poor will suffer at the end. Let, I think, Agrwal write on the labor as such.

I am of the view that an accumulative quantum of the labor used in each process of manufacturing inclusive of labor utilized on the parts as well as raw material for the manufacturing / growth of a production and service may be considered as labor utilized as such, and thereby the price of the commodities / production may be determined. The price determining of a production / commodity despite based on expenditure as such, done on the basis of labor utilized as such will result a complete upside down in the macro and micro economics in the courtiers and the in global economy. This is already practiced in the software industry whose commodities and services are priced on the basis of labor used as such inclusive of non-labor expenditures as well as invocation cost; however excluding expenditure factor from pricing and solely being based on utilized labor as such will also be an economic as such. Besides, this will alien the legitimacy of the people's right on natural resources. Because natural resources and labor together produce commodities, therefore excluding natural resource's cost instead economically value it through labor consumed it will make this notion of Agrawal in contradiction with his Schema, therefore, Agrawal himself will be best person to write on this of his notion in the light of economic justice.

In anyway, everything has to have an economic value – labor or love both. Therefore, ultimately again economic value of accumulated labor used will be valued in economic terms, which has monitory face. Therefore, a Das Labor is required in Agarwal's opinion which has to be in accordance with his schema, which will be in fact Darwinhood in the world economy. A modern Marxism will in fact get birth.

Besides, Agrawal should also write on the two aspects of the commodity and its price determination: (a) the import and other similar taxes on the raw materials, parts and semi-manufactured as well as finally manufactured or produced commodities in the context of wealth, and (b) such taxation's use as cost factor for price determination of a commodity or production.

What Agrawal has not written is the use of cheap labor from developing and underdeveloped world for the manufacturing and services. The industrialists must be taxed at least moderately for acquiring cheap labor, and ensuring distribution of it among those cheap laborers although it is a reality that high population countries like China and India have become beneficiaries for creating the new employment opportunities for their unemployed citizens. Why not a taxes free import economy be part of Agrawal's doctrine to further make agree the wealthy for one-tax on the wealth? This will also lead the protectionist economic approach to an end, and will create a fiscal globalization in the world. This will kick off the process of globalization for the poor and laborer as well. Besides, achieving the goal of development through tax free imports in a country, the attraction for industrialists for that economy will increase that will cause new industrial and urban societies in the world – provided that this is done as part of Agrawal's Line of Wealth doctrine, which ensure surplus financial resources for the governance only through domestic taxes and discuss around GDP of a country.

There approach, where Agrawal is ultra-pro poor in the context of "interest" on the loan, when he says the loaning persons and institutions should not be given right to collect interest. This will be an economic injustice because why a person should lend if he does not receive the cost of the opportunities he lose in the form of investment profit or bank interest benefits. This will end the banking sector of the economy. He in fact, in this context is similar to Islamic tenants on the interest. He rather become Tolstoian in this context when he writes lending should only be for the general good of troubled person; however when he writes regarding business loan, he is absolutely write that investors include in the price of a commodity the payable interest to lender, therefore for interest on the loan should also undergo the structural formula of its distribution. In fact, no mechanism, so far practical reality is concerned, can be there to ensure that an investor does not include the payable interest in the price of the commodities. Simply because of the one principle -- market will decide the sale of a commodity no matter whether it has moderate price or expensive.